FASHION
MARKETING
COMMUNICATIONS

FASHION
MARKETING
COMMUNICATIONS

GAYNOR LEA-GREENWOOD

WILEY

John Wiley & Sons, Ltd.

Registered office

John Wiley & Sons Ltd, The Atrium, Southern Gate, Chichester, West Sussex, PO19 8SQ,
United Kingdom

For details of our global editorial offices, for customer services and for information about how to
apply for permission to reuse the copyright material in this book please see our website at
www.wiley.com.

Images
Figure 2.1 (page 14) courtesy of Adidas; Figure 2.2 (page 15) © ANDREAS SOLARO/AFP/
Getty Images; Figure 3.1a (page 25) © Joe Corrigan/Getty Images; Figure 3.1b (page 25) © 2009
Bloomberg Finance LP; Figure 4.2 (page 49) courtesy of Grazia; Figure 5.1 (page 65) courtesy of
Rimmel; Figure 5.2 (page 66) courtesy of Bastyan; Figure 8.1 (page 119) © 2009 Eric Ryan; Figure
8.5a (page 124) Design by Ada Zanditon; Figure 9.1 (page 144) courtesy of L'Officiel; Figures 11.1
(pages 169–170), 11.2 (page 173) and 11.3 (page 174) courtesy of ALBAM and Red C Marketing;
Figure 12.1 (page 185): courtesy of Garance Dore

Thanks to: Incu, Albam, JDSports, redcmarketing, zcussons, bastyan, rimmel, JWT, indali, and jaeger for
providing visuals.

Library of Congress Cataloging-in-Publication Data

A catalogue record for this book is available from the British Library.
ISBN 978-1-405-15060-6 (paperback) ISBN 978-1-118-49617-6 (ebk)
ISBN 978-1-118-49615-2 (ebk) ISBN 978-1-118-49616-9 (ebk)

Set in 11/15pt Gill Sans std by MPS Limited, Chennai, India
Printed and bound in Singapore by Markono Print Media Pte Ltd

CONTENTS

Chapter 7 The Retail Fashion Store Environment

ACKNOWLEDGMENTS

I am really indebted to those of you who helped, you know who you are and . . . to those who didn't, you know who you are and I do too. Seriously, I am grateful to all at Wiley-Blackwell, both past and present, for pushing me through the pain barrier. It has taken forever, I know.

Inspiration over the years has come from a wide variety of sources:

- my nan, who introduced me to the frustrating concept of window shopping, when the shops were shut
- my parents, who let me buy and hoard magazines and clothes, in their space, long after I had left home, who also encouraged and supported my choice of career, first in the 'rag trade' and then lecturing
- my visits to international fashion destinations for business or pleasure
- students past and present for looking like they were listening to my stories, during lectures, then telling me their stories
- the fashion industry for being a constant source of interest and indeed joy
- moleskine notebooks with lots of lists
- displacement activities, too many to mention
- my sister Madeleine and my friend Barbara for a lot of laughs along the way.

Dedication: this is for my son Max. May this little book keep you in the manner to which you have become accustomed or, if not, remind you of me sitting at the kitchen table writing, whilst you just brought me your dirty washing, asked if I'd had another 'productive day' in a sarcastic manner and then asked what was for tea. It was never going to be the Harry Potter or blockbuster equivalent for which you had hoped.

Now, having finally finished this, I am off on another shopping trip. Do your own washing and make your own tea, Max!

My dear Mum would have been thrilled and organised a book launch.

—Gaynor Lea-Greenwood
April 2012

1

INTRODUCTION

I was the author of Chapter 9 in the seminal and popular textbook, *Fashion Marketing*, edited by Mike Easey, which is currently in its third edition. This book is a response to a request for more on fashion marketing communications (FMC) at a time of growing interest in the subject as a distinct and yet integral part of the fashion industry. It has also come from my own needs as a lecturer in the subject of fashion marketing communications. Need is the mother of invention, as the saying goes.

For me, and probably for others, the interest in FMC was driven by traditional and online content in magazines; an exponential growth in PR, including advertorials, editorials, product placement, sponsorship and bloggers; pop-up stores; the cult of celebrity and the rise of social media. This has coincided with an economic downturn, in which 'getting more bang for your buck' is a key issue. The book was also conceived when 'fast fashion' was at its zenith. It also reflects the wider range of roles that students and fashion professionals are taking up in the industry.

So, the starting point of this book has been a long interest in the literature on marketing communications and finding, in my teaching of fashion marketing, that there was nothing really tailored to my needs. I cannot by any means say that I am an expert in the area of marketing communications but I have adapted seminal works to my interests in fashion and to my teaching purposes. I expect that some of you using this book have done the same.

Description of the book

I assume some level of knowledge, so that this text will fit with lecturers and students: having developed and understood the concept of the marketing mix, both audiences (lecturers and students) are now looking for details of the promotional mix to apply to FMC.

'Fashion marketing communications' and 'promotion' are terms that I use interchangeably; in some cases, FMC encompasses a wider and more professional remit than the traditional 'promotional mix' with which we may all be familiar.

This book follows a typical lecture schedule for an academic year of one or two terms or semesters, with some seminar input and student-focused exercises.

It, therefore, includes activities and some further reading. I hope these can be adapted by lecturers as appropriate.

I also hope that lecturers and students can use this book as a starting point, because it is by no means all-encompassing. By its very nature, fashion is about change and the fashion industry is different from many other industries; by the time you are reading this, things will have developed further. However, what has happened in the past is relevant for a historical understanding or underpinning of how we got to where we are today and, perhaps more importantly, why.

I know now why fashion is so under-represented in the academic literature found in text books and even journal articles (with their shorter lead times); they are often seen as outmoded because, as is the nature of fashion, it's all about change and obsolescence.

Structure of the book

The layout of each chapter follows the same format: chapter objectives; an introduction; a definition, if it is required; explanation and examples of the major themes and content; a summary; ideas for activities that can easily be adapted; and further reading, which can be a starting point for further research. There are also some in-depth case studies, which can be used at any stage in a programme.

Most terminology is explained within the text because many students will 'switch off' if they do not get an explanation immediately. Lecturers and students always like to start with a definition to set the scene; formal definitions don't always exist, so I have created them.

In Chapter 2, the book attempts to start at the beginning of the communications process, with the role of strategy in FMC: understanding where a company is now and wants to be in the future. This is fundamental to establishing promotional objectives that lead to promotional activities. I am acutely aware that an 'emergent strategy' is often the one which best suits what I have called the 'fast and fickle' nature of the fashion business in a busy, cluttered and extremely competitive retail fashion environment. There are many books on general business strategy but none solely on FMC strategy so, for the purposes of this chapter, the major themes and concepts of strategy are applied to fashion communications.

Chapter 3 identifies the major tools of communication relevant to fashion retailing and marketing communications. Despite an exponential growth in social media during the writing of this book, traditional tools (such as magazines and PR) are still as important.

Despite new technology, no other channel has been able to display the luxury and elegance of print ads like magazines.

—'Tatler tries on augmented reality to celebrate
September Web relaunch', www.luxurydaily.com, I August 2011

The tools and media channels available are discussed in terms of their advantages and disadvantages, as I find this is a useful way to analyse their relative merits. Students seem to like this checklist approach.

I make no apology for giving television advertising a wide berth. There are many texts that deal with television advertising but it is seldom used by fashion retailers (although highly targeted satellite channels, such as MTV, do have opportunities for wider exposure and 'reach' in fashion promotion), so I merely touch on it.

Chapter 4 looks at our emotional connection with magazines, how they work and what fashion consumers get from them in terms of a combination of information and entertainment, called 'infotainment'. Magazines are often considered as a 'light and fluffy' aspect of fashion but I suggest that they remain a major communication channel, whether in glossy, two-dimensional, 'have and hold' format or in online content or moving both forward in parallel.

Chapter 5 looks in detail at public relations (PR), including product placement and the role of PR in various media and how it might be valued more robustly. PR was (until relatively recently) widely regarded as a poor relation to traditional promotional channels such as advertising. Chapter 5 demonstrates how important the role has become in a crowded and cluttered media environment; where the role of editorial acts as a credible source of information, particularly for the fashion consumer.

Chapter 6 discusses the role of celebrity in fashion marketing communications. Despite the various announcements that celebrity culture has become 'tired' or is 'dead', the evidence in society and the media does not support this. A model of the celebrity lifecycle is introduced.

Chapter 7 makes no apologies for being a long chapter about the role of communications within the retail environment itself. Visual merchandising and the whole in-store experience that affects purchasing decisions is renamed 'visual marketing'. This is because I feel that this element in communications has not been covered in enough depth and rigour in relation to a holistic approach to marketing communications. It is much more important than simply 'dressing dummies'. This chapter also considers the difficulties of translating the in-store experience into an online experience.

Chapter 8 considers the role of trade marketing communications, that is, business-to-business (B2B) rather than business-to-consumer (B2C) communications. Much of the fashion industry is concerned with wholesaling and supplying the retail trade and this is an area which has hitherto been neglected. This chapter attempts to demonstrate the difference in communication strategy and tools, with a generally more knowledgeable trade or industry audience.

Chapter 9 takes a look at internationalisation in FMC and sets many of the preceding themes within the international context. This is most apposite considering the various push and pull factors that are driving fashion into the international arena.

Chapter 10 examines the often combatorial relationship that fashion promotion has with the regulatory frameworks that exist in many developed markets. This is not surprising, as fashion is associated with symbols of sex and issues of size, airbrushing, the sexualisation of minors and nudity. This will be a continuing tension as fashion so often reflects contemporary culture.

Chapter 11 looks at how the effectiveness of FMC can be measured. This has been a particularly difficult chapter to write; to this day, I do not know whether anyone has discovered a complete answer to this question. I describe some methodologies, but who actually knows what goes on in the 'black box' of the subconscious? Many people have tried but all have failed to make a rational or foolproof case for what can be considered totally irrational behaviour in fashion purchasing and the influence of marketing communications in fashion purchasing decisions.

Chapter 12 contains some career guidance for people entering the fashion marketing communications industry. Knowing, understanding and being able to use the terminology is vital to demonstrating interest in the area. Work experience in whatever capacity is necessary and this begins with research, observation and an appropriate CV.

2

MARKETING STRATEGY

If we fail to plan then we plan to fail.

—Anonymous

THIS CHAPTER:

↳ outlines the starting point for companies when faced with a competitive environment

↳ explains what strategy is in fashion marketing communications

↳ explains the models and tools of strategy

↳ gives examples of companies' strategies.

Introduction

Put simply, a strategy is an overarching plan for long-, medium- or short-term achievement of the company's objectives.

Corporate strategy tends to be long term and is often incorporated in the mission statement issued by an organisation in their communications with the public (customers, employees and shareholders). Its objective is to sum up the essence of what the company is and what it stands for. The following mission statement is for a company that sells family fashion at value prices:

To be a major player in fashion for the family, offering convenience, choice, value and quality

---

A corporate strategy should guide all aspects of an organisation's operations, into what are called functional strategies – product selection, price architecture, distribution and promotional activities. The functional strategies incorporate all aspects of the marketing mix in order to fulfil the corporate strategy. To fulfil the statement above, the company will select products that match the target market's desire for quality fashion at affordable prices, available in high-street shops and online.

When product, price and place (or distribution, for example, shops or online outlets) are correctly managed, then the organisation can look at creating a promotional strategy. In the example, the functional promotional strategy would probably include television advertising.

The various acronyms introduced in this chapter are useful for memorising the parts of the process but they do not necessarily reflect industry practice or the reality of promotional planning.

Promotional strategy

Promotion is a term that is often used interchangeably with 'marketing communications'.

The promotional mix consists of:

- ✎ **advertising**
- ✎ **sales promotion**
- ✎ **personal selling**
- ✎ **public relations**
- ✎ **direct marketing**

The specific usage of each of these items is elucidated in Chapter 3; for now, we consider them in general terms.

- ✎ **Advertising** is considered to be 'above the line' activity, which means that it is clear to the consumer where the information originates from. It consists of paid-for communications from company to company or consumer.
- ✎ **Sales promotions** are in-store activities, which may include short-term discounts to stimulate demand.
- ✎ **Personal selling** is the use of sales personnel to communicate with potential customers.
- ✎ **Public relations** refers to less obvious forms of promotion, such as product placement in magazines, sometimes called 'below the line' activity as it is not always clear what originates with the company and what is editorial comment.
- ✎ **Direct marketing** consists of mail shots and, more recently, e-mail, SMS communications and immediate links to purchase, such as quick response (QR) codes.

Promotion should be integrated with the rest of the marketing mix. No amount of communications can sell a product which is not wanted by the consumer, is not at the right price point or is not readily available.

For any strategy, and it is no different with promotional strategy, there are three fundamental questions:

- ✎ Where are we now?
- ✎ Where do we want to be?
- ✎ How do we get there or achieve it?

Deceptively, these appear to be simple questions. Their complexity should not be underrated or you will come up with simplistic answers.

We can expand this model to cover the whole promotional cycle with the acronym **SOSTAC:**

- ↳ **Situation analysis** (where are we now?)
- ↳ **Objectives** (where do we want to be?)
- ↳ **Strategies** (how do we get there?)
- ↳ **Tactics** (which tools do we use?)
- ↳ **Activities, actions and analysis** (what we do and how we measure it)
- ↳ **Control** (evaluation of activities and feedback).

Where are we now?

A brand-new company is unknown to the target market and its promotional strategy starts from a very low base: it has no profile and no previous perceptions. The start-up costs of promotional activity can be extremely expensive from this position as awareness of the company, brand and their product is non-existent. However, changing the public's perception of an existing brand is considered much harder to do. Perceptions and attitudes towards a brand are sometimes so firmly established in a consumer's mind that it takes a very expensive and sustained promotional campaign to make even a small shift in attitude.

An existing company must carry out a *situational audit*. This means undertaking research to attempt to understand the competitive environment and the perceptions of the brand held by past and present consumers. It also entails analysing previous and existing campaigns.

Such research can be undertaken by the company itself, if it has the skills. However, it is much more likely to be done by a professional research company or an advertising agency.

In the late 1990s, French Connection discovered via research that the brand was no longer 'salient'. In other words, it was no longer uppermost in the consumer's mind. French Connection had lost its market position due to a number of factors, not least new entrants to the market and existing competition.

Where do we want to be?

Based on the research into its current position, a company can move towards setting realistic, precise and achievable objectives, such as:

↳ Introduce the brand to the market using a full campaign that integrates advertising across all available media channels.

↳ Raise consumer awareness of the brand amongst the core target market by targeting the media used by the core consumer.

↳ Drive sales through reducing prices in sales promotions in store, in magazines and online.

↳ Create exciting selling environments by refitting the retail environment.

↳ Deliver a quality–value proposition to customers that confirms low prices but good quality.

These are viable objectives that can lead to a functional or operational specific strategy.

Objectives of the promotional mix should be **SMART:**

↳ **Specific,** for example, to increase sales

↳ **Measurable,** for example, any increase in sales can be identified

↳ **Achievable,** for example, a discount coupon will encourage customers

↳ **Relevant,** for example, a discount coupon will be welcome in a recession

↳ **Timed,** for example, the campaign will run over specific dates.

French Connection decided to reposition the company as an edgy brand. Repositioning a company is about changing consumer perceptions and is often extremely expensive as it involves a great deal of promotional effort. French Connection wanted to communicate that it was an edgy urban brand but, because of falling sales, the campaign had to be done on a small budget. It did this by using 'fcuk' in slogans on T-shirts ('fcuk fashion' was the first one and was an instant sell out).

Customers were paying to advertise the brand out on the streets. Every time a new version of the fcuk slogan was released, it was considered relevant to the target market, which enjoyed the iconic and cheeky slogans. The increased sales were both achievable and measurable. This was a very successful and cost-effective campaign – French Connection advertised solely on billboards, which are considerably cheaper than television or magazine advertising. The revenue from the sales of the T-shirts allowed French Connection to expand into international markets and new product categories (toiletries, fragrance) based on the return on the low promotional investment.

However, it became apparent over time that the consumer grew tired of the 'fcuk' innovation – it became stale. The idea of using the T-shirt as a tool of promotion should probably have been time limited.

How do we get there?

The choice of strategy must be realistic. For example, if sales are falling, it is unlikely that a single expensive TV advertising campaign promoting the store will either be financially viable or stimulate demand in the long term: the rest of the mix must be addressed.

The strategy must consider the **five Ms** involved:

- **Muscle, or men (and women)** – the people to undertake the activities
- **Money** – the budget for the activities
- **Minutes** – how much time will be allocated for the activities
- **Message** – the promotional message
- **Measurement** – how results will be measured.

Fashion promotion in a competitive environment must stand out from the bigger players with their large budgets. The main objective of the luxury brands is to stay in the consumer's mind so they advertise continually with their distinctive image as their theme. In contrast, most middle-market fashion brands do not have this type of budget. New designers and independent retailers also do not have large budgets for promotional campaigns.

An 'evoked set' refers to the brands which come first to consumers' minds when they are asked where they shop; they are also known as a consumer's 'repertoire' of brands. If sales are falling and the rest of the mix appears attractive to the target market but research has shown that the brand does not register in the consumer's mind, this would suggest the need for a promotional mix to create awareness. Budgetary constraints may make it appropriate to increase below-the-line activity:

- Link up with a charity
- Develop celebrity endorsement
- Sponsor a fashion event
- Increase product placement
- Upgrade the website to include video content
- Encourage bloggers to discuss the brand.

To achieve these objectives, a company may hire a public relations (PR) agency or develop in-house PR skills to gain coverage of these activities in the press.

If the brand has the finance, then a complete campaign including both advertising and PR activities may be appropriate.

French Connection did not have a large budget so they simply used the fcuk name (the abbreviation of French Connection UK). The 'fcuk' campaign got the brand talked about because it used what was called 'dyslexic daring'. It also managed to get a lot of free press coverage.

Models of advertising

A model is a simple way of explaining a complex process (think of the reality of the London underground compared with the simplicity of the model – the map).

One of the earliest models of how advertising works is the **AIDA** model, a linear model of a complex process that attempts to demonstrate how a consumer moves from awareness to purchase. The model suggests that consumers pass through four stages before making a purchase:

- ↳ **Awareness** or knowledge (cognition): The consumer becomes aware of a brand or product as a result of one or more elements of a communication campaign: advertising, online communications, in-store promotions, PR or billboards.
- ↳ **Interest** (affect): The consumer responds positively and likes what they see or hear.
- ↳ **Desire:** The consumer wants to try the product or purchase the product.
- ↳ **Action:** The consumer moves towards an intention to buy.

Advertising can create awareness, interest can be generated by editorial coverage, desire can be created by favourable editorial comment and the move to action can be facilitated by a discount, a mobile phone application or a website link.

Examples of promotional campaigns

When the budget is low, innovative ideas can reap rewards.

Harold Crabtree is an independent, family-owned, upper-market fashion retailer with only two branches, one in a market town and one in a larger nearby town.

The company would not be able to afford, fulfil nor sustain the demand if it were featured in *Vogue*. However, it took out a small classified advertisement at the back of the magazine for a modest sum and can now proudly boast on in-store show cards that they have been 'seen in *Vogue*'. It is essentially true.

Wonderbra used oversized billboards and a relatively unknown (and therefore cheap) model to re-launch itself, gaining free press coverage.

When the budget is low, integration is key: one image and its initial costs (for photography, the model, make-up, hair, etc.) can go a long way. A company can gain economies of scale by using the same image across all the media channels it utilises: a magazine advert can be repeated in store, on billboards, on leaflets and on a website.

Adidas is well known as a global player with a substantial promotional spend. It also resorts to economies of scale and budgetary manipulation. David Beckham is one of their celebrity brand ambassadors but his time is expensive, so one advert is photographed and is then 'coloured up' to suggest that a number of garments and shots are being featured (see Figure 2.1). This makes the campaign appear fresh and different for each publication yet achieves the economies of replication.

When budgets are constrained, there may be a very great temptation to use shock tactics to get the brand talked about in the wider media. Companies will vehemently deny this but there may linger a healthy note of cynicism in this

Figure 2.1 Recoloured Adidas advert

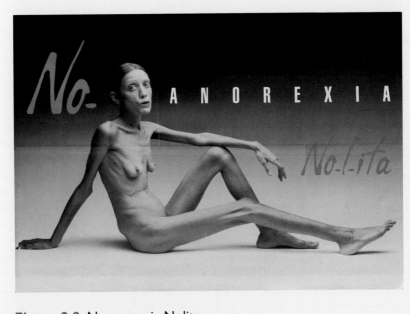

Figure 2.2 No anorexia Nolita

respect. Benetton is probably the most well-known example of using shock tactics. As every advert was released, it was banned; eventually every advert was vetted before publication. Benetton also got more free press coverage.

An unknown brand, Nolita got unprecedented media coverage in 2007 by using an anorexic-looking model in its campaign (see Figure 2.2) at the height of the size zero debate, which still continues today.

Summary

A clear, widely known and understood strategy within the company will ensure that the company knows where it is now, knows where it wants to be and all parts of the whole are working towards getting there.

This chapter has:

- ✍ outlined the promotional mix available to an organisation
- ✍ explained some strategic tools and models in marketing communications
- ✍ given examples of a variety of budgetary constraints when formulating strategy.

References

Copley, P. (2004) *Marketing Communications Management*, Elsevier, Oxford.

Egan, J. (2007) *Marketing Communications*, Thomson Learning, London.

Fill, C. (2007) *Marketing Communications*, Butterworth-Heinemann, Oxford.

Hackley, C. (2005) *Advertising and Promotion*, Sage, London.

Kapferer, J. N. and Bastien, V. (2009) *The Luxury Strategy*, Kogan Page, London.

Lea-Greenwood, G. (2008) 'Fashion Marketing Communications' in M. Easey (ed.), *Fashion Marketing*, 3rd edition, Blackwell Science, Oxford.

Activities

1 Select a company and analyse its promotional tools. Consider what strategies it appears to be using and why.
2 Find advertisements, in-store posters, product placement or direct-marketing tools that appear to use the same or a slightly manipulated image for economies of scale and integration.

3

TOOLS AND MEDIA CHANNELS

A poor workman blames his tools.

—Traditional

THIS CHAPTER:

↳ explores the marketing communications tools available to companies

↳ explains the advantages and disadvantages of each tool and media channel

↳ gives examples of tools and media channels in the fashion industry.

Introduction

Once research has been carried out, objectives have been set and a strategy has been determined, we can choose tools and media channels to achieve success. In this chapter, we consider the tools and media channels we should use. We also consider where, when and why we should use them.

Some of the tools and media channels that we consider deserve chapters of their own due to their importance in the fashion industry. Chapter 4 considers magazines; Chapter 5 discusses public relations; Chapter 6 discusses the role of celebrity endorsement; Chapter 7 considers the retail environment; and Chapter 8 discusses trade marketing.

The tools of the promotional mix are sometimes simply described as:

- advertising
- public relations
- direct marketing
- personal selling.

The nature of integration means that there is a great deal of overlap and cross-fertilisation between the four tools of communication. One department or agency may oversee all of the company's communications.

However, the nature of fashion marketing causes us to add the following tools:

- the retail environment
- viral, web communications and social media.

Increasingly the distinct categories of the promotional mix have become blended and you must take an integrated approach to using the elements.

Advertising

By 'advertising', we mean any form of outward-facing communication that is clearly seen to come from a company. It is usually paid for and originates with the company. It includes advertising in the following media:

- television (terrestrial and satellite)
- cinema

- magazine and newspaper
- radio
- outdoor and transport
- Internet.

The choice of a particular medium and the cost of an advertisement (known as an 'advert') in that medium is dictated by the number of people who will see, read, watch or listen to the advert.

Costs associated with each of these types of advertising can be accessed via the website of a specific media channel or publication. These costs are for the media space and do not reflect the costs associated with shooting a campaign. When exotic destinations, celebrity photographers, models and stylists are factored in, the costs can be extremely high.

Somewhere between advertisements and public relations come 'advertorials'. An advertorial is where a company takes a whole page and asks a journalist to discuss the company and product in a style which is more like editorial commentary than a straightforward advertisement. The company clearly sponsors the space but a celebrity, stylist, or expert may confirm the attributes of the brand. Advertorials are neither 'above' nor 'below' the line (see Chapter 2); they are sometimes referred to as 'across' or 'on' the line. It may be worth noting that the notion of a 'line' is becoming increasingly blurred and should really be dropped now.

Advertising on mobile devices crosses the divide into direct marketing.

Television advertising

TV advertising has a wide *reach*, which means that it can be seen by a lot of people from a wide variety of demographics (a 'demographic' describes the characteristics of an audience in terms of age, gender or life stage). TV advertising tends to be expensive in terms of professional production costs and the most sought-after media slots (the ones in the commercial breaks of the most popular TV shows) are also expensive to occupy.

TV adverts need to appeal to a large majority of viewers. They are, therefore, more suited to retailers and brands that have a wide geographic and demographic spread, such as Marks and Spencer (M&S), Gap, Nike and Levi's.

TV advertising can utilise music and movement to good effect: it is three dimensional and can attract attention but normally it only lasts between 30 and 60 seconds. It cannot show a whole range of products but needs to focus on a narrow presentation and on image building. Levi's iconic advert, set in a laundrette with the background music *Heard It Through the Grapevine*, only showed the 501 style of jeans. It created such demand that stores ran out of 501s.

TV can stimulate demand so strongly that it is important that buyers and merchandisers are involved in the process at an early stage to ensure availability of the product and avoid disappointing the consumer. On the other hand, consumers may perceive that the product is too popular – they don't want to look like everyone else.

Consumers can use 'selective perception', which means that they do not pay attention to an advertisement which does not appear relevant to them. They may 'tune out' or channel hop during adverts or they may edit their viewing (by using replay features that allow a programme to be watched without the advertisements), but a strong 'musical worm' can capture their attention. A musical worm is an audible logo or symbol, for example, jingles that you immediately identify with an advert or brand when you hear them. Intel has a musical worm.

TV adverts can be cost effective in an integrated campaign where 'stills' are replicated on billboards, in magazines and in store. However, that can saturate the media environment and the consumer can become bored or tired with seeing the same pictures.

TV advertising can be targeted to the composition of the audience. The ad break in the UK's most popular soap, *Coronation Street*, is the most expensive advertising slot on a regular basis. One-off TV specials, such as interviews with royalty or celebrities, can also command high prices and there is much competition for them. It is important for the TV ratings that the viewer does not switch to a different channel during the ad break and stay there, so adverts have to be relevant to the audience.

With the decline in the numbers of people watching terrestrial TV, the cost of advertising has steadily been decreasing. This has allowed, for example, H&M to enter the arena, where in the past the advertising costs may have been too high

and the audience might not have been as easy to define. Specialised TV programmes, shown on either terrestrial or satellite channels, about fashion, modelling
and what to wear or reality competitions can be competitively priced and target a
specific demographic. These programmes can be very attractive to advertisers as
the majority of the audience will be in the target market.

TV advertising of one-off special sales for department stores is most commonly
aired the night before the sale. It appears to drive consumer action.

Cinema advertising

Cinema advertising can use an extended version of a TV advert (or a more
explicit version, if the audience is over 18). A longer version can communicate
more on image and product range. Cinema's target market can be more precisely
defined because certain films (action, comedy or romance) appeal to separate
segments of the total population. Product placement in a film can be reflected
in the advertising. Cinema advertising can reflect the local geography, advertising
local fashion malls, but some local advertising can be very unprofessional or ama-
teurish and merely draw hoots of derision.

The release of the film *The Devil Wears Prada* offered an opportunity for luxury
brands to show their location. Chanel No 5 re-used the Nicole Kidman advert
one year after its original launch. Chanel was name-checked continually throughout the film and there was prominent product placement as it was Chanel clothing and accessories that the geeky assistant chose to transform herself into a
fashionista.

A cinema audience is somewhat captive as people have paid to watch the film.
To a certain extent, they are more attentive than a TV audience; however this
may increase their resistance as they are impatient for the film to start and they
may spend the advertising time getting popcorn, settling down and talking (and
disturbing others). Some people may only arrive at the start of the film.

Cinema advertising can be more impressive on a big screen rather than a TV
screen. It can be longer and more effective in communicating, using film-like
techniques. Indeed, one sometimes thinks a film or a trailer is starting but it is
a cinematic treatment of advertising. It is no surprise that many famous film
directors gained their first experience of the medium through directing iconic

ads. *Fight Club* director David Fincher has directed iconic ads for Nike, Levi's and Adidas.

Cinema may prove useful to test advertising before it rolls out nationally. Audiences are often the subject of marketing research after a film.

Magazine advertising

For fashion retailers and brands, magazine advertising is the most effective form of advertising relative to cost as it can be highly targeted to the magazine's readership.

The position of an advert is extremely important because of the way in which consumers 'browse' magazines and use them for a combination of news features and trends. We discuss this in more detail in Chapter 4.

Magazines use good colour reproduction, which is vital for fashion advertising, and are printed on glossy paper (indeed, they are often called the 'glossies'). Magazine adverts can reinforce advertising which has been in another media as it can replicate a still from a TV advert, which reminds the reader very quickly of the original.

The major fashion publications are expensive for advertisers, compared to newspapers, but are deemed to be worth the cost because of their reach (they are read, re-read and passed on). In the context of magazines, 'reading' might mean 'perusing' or 'flicking through' a number of times, which increases the consumer's exposure to advertising.

Newspaper advertising

Newspapers can be daily, weekly, national or local and therefore can be useful for reaching different audiences and achieving different objectives. Unlike magazines, newspapers are discarded as soon as they have been read, so immediate action is an objective of this advertising channel.

Fashion companies can advertise one-day sales with the immediacy of today or tomorrow and show product examples. Coupons can also be cut out and redeemed. Readers can be directed to company websites.

Newspapers are mostly black and white so colour, when used, does stand out. With digital printing, it is now cheaper and sharper.

Newspapers may be read selectively by different members of a household: men may turn to the sports pages, women to features and fashion, so the positioning of the advertising is an important consideration. The choice and price of a particular position is dictated by the number of people who will see and read the advert.

Newspaper advertising can be targeted towards the readership. For example *The Financial Times* and *The Wall Street Journal* will attract a certain strata of professional society and the advertising will be highly targeted towards their needs and interests, such as business attire.

Newspaper readership is in decline due to the availability of news 24/7 on the Internet. However, weekend colour supplements (such as the *FT*'s 'How to Spend it' and *The Sunday Times* 'Style' section has given newspaper advertising a new channel to consumers. These supplements are not kept as long as magazines, but are perused in the same way as magazines to take in trend and celebrity information.

Radio advertising

Radio as a communication channel provides a number of opportunities but, on the whole, it has more disadvantages for most advertisers, in particular fashion companies. Radio cannot provide a visual stimulus but a mnemonic (for example, a catchy tune or 'worm') may work just as well if associated with a store or brand.

One-off special events, such as sales, can be promoted but the radio does tend to be what people call 'shouty' to try and grab attention – the Advertising Standards Authority has observed that the volume often increases during advertisements and this is within what is already a noisy environment.

Local radio can provide opportunities for local stores to advertise but the polish and professionalism may not be there. However, radio is relatively cheap compared to other media.

Outdoor ambient media

Billboards along roads and at busy traffic intersections are often used by companies as an advertising tool. However, they should not distract pedestrians or drivers (distractions might cause accidents), therefore they tend not to have much text. They may only be given a glance but can remind customers embarking on a shopping trip that the brand exists, especially if the same image has been used in magazines or if a still from a TV advert is replicated, as this reinforces previous exposure.

Matalan uses billboards on main roads near to their out-of-town stores. This may prompt a motorist to visit the store.

Billboard advertising is relatively cheap depending on the location. See the websites of JC Decaux or any outdoor media owner for details. Billboards may need refreshing frequently as motorists tend to use the same route to work. They can also be subject to wear and tear of the weather or from graffiti artists. Modern technology has developed digital billboard advertising in which paper poster sheets are replaced by electronic screens. These are growing in popularity and they can be changed on a daily basis or even at different times of the day. They have movement, which attracts attention.

Transport ambient media

Whilst waiting for public transport (in metro, underground or train stations and at bus shelters), the commuter is a 'captive' audience and may be looking for a distraction. On the other hand, they are bombarded by promotions within these environments and may actively screen them out (selective perception) or read a book. Many commuters board and alight at the same place on a daily basis, so advertisers may need to change their promotions more frequently – familiarity will make the viewer switch off or screen out.

Taxis, buses and other forms of public transport are used widely as advertising channels as they cover a lot of ground (see Figure 3.1). Popular routes, such as through the main shopping districts, will cost more than those in rural or out-of-town locations. However, it must be noted that the route that a bus takes should be appropriate for the content. Some have been criticised by the advertising standards authority as being too risqué.

Figure 3.1 Advertising on a bus and a taxi

Internet advertising

A company website is a form of advertising which consumers may actively seek out. Most media channels now give a web address as a contact point. Pop-up adverts can be intrusive and annoying.

The consumer can now sign up for e-mail alerts and mobile applications from a brand; this is a form of active rather than passive engagement with the brand; however companies need to ensure that they collect and use consumer details in a responsible and targeted manner. Consumers will unsubscribe and have a negative attitude towards a company that passes their details on without permission or gets their name, interests or family composition wrong.

Amazon, whilst not an example from the fashion industry, can be seen as particularly effective. When a customer returns to their website, Amazon suggests other products purchased by customers who bought the same item. More often than not Amazon is accurate in its buying behaviour observations, as can be evidenced if you have purchased from Amazon. Net-a-porter also does this effectively and other fashion companies could learn from these examples with their selections and tailor their alerts to the consumer.

SMS (text message) communications are another example of technology being a central tool in marketing communications. When these communications are targeted and welcome, it is a useful reminder; when they are not then it becomes intrusive.

Public relations

Public relations (PR) is a means by which companies attempt to influence consumer opinion about their marketing mix, image or ethos. PR is a subtle and less obvious form of promotion than advertising. To the untrained eye or ear, it may sound like an influential style leader is recommending the brand. The information originates with the company but its end use is in the hands of the journalists using the press packs, releases and sample garments.

PR is particularly relevant for the fashion industry as consumers use trend leaders and stylists as a source of information and inspiration about trends, especially when looking at magazines and blogs.

Public relations activities can include:

- **press relationships,** which are vital as the press come to rely on the PR function for samples and stories
- **press releases,** which PR use to alert the media to brands, stories, new collections and events
- **sponsorship and celebrity management** (see Chapter 6 for more detail)
- **product placement**
- **events management** for the public or journalists
- **crisis management,** which on occasion involves responding to negative publicity
- **guerrilla campaigns,** which can be relatively inexpensive as consumers pass on coupons or viral ads
- **pop-up stores**
- **social media,** such as Facebook, fan sites and blogs.

Product placement

The major advantage of placing products in editorial pieces, with celebrities and in magazine fashion shoots is that of credibility. The average fashion consumer is not aware that there is a huge publicity machine driving the placement of fashion items in the media, whether worn by presenters or celebrities, in daytime TV programmes, in films or in glossy magazines. Magazines may include features such as 'The best little black dress for this season'. In-house or external PR agencies provide these items. The average fashion consumer believes that the stylist or editorial team have selected these items personally to showcase to their readers; the reality is somewhat different.

The disadvantages can be that the product may not be shown in a good light. For example, a cheaper version may be shown alongside it. However any publicity can be good publicity – the fashion consumer knows there are 'minted' (luxury) and 'skinted' (high street) versions of each trend.

The additional demand that can be ignited due to shrewd product placement can be a disadvantage: the retailer may not have the merchandise and distribution channels to fulfil customers' requirements. This can lead to dissatisfaction and negative attitudes. To prevent this, it is important that companies, magazines and retail outlets are all kept abreast of information which is going into the public domain.

In some cases, editorial coverage may be given to a product which is no longer available or was never stocked outside of London. It may have been chosen from a bank of images to match a theme on a page. This can be very frustrating for the potential customer.

The value of product placement, whilst not an exact science, is roughly calculated by the industry as being three times more than the value of a traditional advert, due to this credibility factor. If someone who is seen as an influential style leader is talking about and recommending your brand, it goes a long way towards a stamp of approval.

Pop-up stores

A *pop-up store* refers to a short-term lease in a location that the retailer might not normally consider or at an exclusive event. Such a store can be very beneficial to a company in testing a location or trialling a new store design in a low-key way that will not damage the main stores. A pop-up store also gains press coverage.

Social networking

Social media has become one of the most important tools for companies in communicating with customers. Instead of a 'push' strategy (where communications are sent to customers in the hope that they will respond favourably), social media can include a 'pull' strategy, in which two-way communication can be established. 'Liking' a brand on Facebook means joining a community of brand fans. These media channels are often run by PR companies. PR agents also trawl blogs to see who is talking about the brand.

Direct marketing

Direct marketing is a tool by which companies target and communicate on a one-to-one basis with a customer (B2C) or another business (B2B) may operate.

Summary

This chapter has outlined the advantages and disadvantages of the communication tools available to fashion companies. The tools seldom work in isolation and are part of an integrated approach to fashion marketing communications.

References

The Devil Wears Prada, film (2006) directed by David Frankel. Fox 2000 Pictures, USA.

Lea-Greenwood, G. (1998) 'Visual merchandising: a neglected area in UK fashion marketing?', *International Journal of Retail & Distribution Management*, 26(8):324–329.

National Skills Academy, *The Guide to Successful Retailing – Inspired by Mary Portas*, www .nsaforretail.com/NSAR/Retailers/GuidetoSuccessfulRetailing/.

Activities

1   Monitor advertising aimed at different segments of the population on terrestrial and satellite TV. Consider programmes that are also directed at clearly defined markets.

2   Visit the cinema and make some observations on the length, sound, creative treatment and subject or brands of the advertising in relation to the film genre.

3   Look at the types of 'fashion' adverts in magazines which are related to hobbies or interests.

4   Select newspapers directed at different audiences and compare the types of advertising.

5   Who tends to advertise on radio stations to which you listen?

6   On your daily commute, make a note of the advertising to which you are exposed over a week or so. At what point do you screen out and what changes do you notice?

7   Subscribe to a number of fashion websites and monitor their communications in general and those focussed on you personally. Do some retailers bombard you with messages? Do some get it about right? Or do they seem to forget that you are interested in them? Do their communications address you and your needs personally?

8   Find a piece of product placement and then, acting as a 'normal' consumer, find the item in a store or on a website. What observations can you make regarding the level of communication between the people involved in getting the media coverage and the store personnel. Do store personnel know it was featured in a magazine? Has it sold out already? Will any more come into stock?

9   Visit a store that you do not normally frequent and make some observations on how the retail environment communicates to a target market that does not include you.

THE
POWER OF
MAGAZINES

4

There's very little advice in men's magazines, because men don't think there's a lot they don't know. Women do. Women want to learn.

—Jerry Seinfeld, chat show host

THIS CHAPTER:

↳ explores the importance of magazines in fashion

↳ explains the relationship consumers have with magazines

↳ explains the relationship between costs, circulation and context

↳ explains the role and value of product placement.

Introduction

Magazines are a fundamental communication tool in fashion marketing; it is overwhelmingly from magazines that fashion consumers learn about new trends, how to wear a trend, what celebrities are wearing and how to get the look for less. Readers also learn some negatives about their style or body shape but magazines advise them on how to overcome problems. Magazines are a trusted source of information: they are style tutors and readers look to them for guidelines.

Between the fashion pages are a few features. Fashion magazines have to have some features, otherwise we would feel that they were too flippant and frivolous. The style, tone and nature of features depend very much on the type of magazine: compare the features in *Vogue* with those of a celebrity weekly.

Magazines have a dual role in helping us solve our fashion crises and entertaining us at the same time. To quote Gloria Steinem, feminist author, magazines are '. . . simply trying to mould women into bigger and better consumers'. Whatever your point of view, fashion magazines are big business: magazines such as *Vogue*, *Grazia*, and *Elle* are global brands in their own right.

Magazines are targeted at very specific segments of the fashion-consuming public; they cannot be all things to all people. They are highly targeted at different types of fashion consumer:

- innovators or early style adopters (e.g. *Vogue*, *POP* and *Face*)
- fashion enthusiasts (e.g. *Grazia*)
- late style adopters (e.g. *Closer* or *More*).

The most popular magazines tend to be found in a shop at eye level and this translates into 'buy' level (see Figure 4.1). A number of publications, mostly weekly or celebrity orientated, now command a special point-of-sale fixture of their own, close to the till. This is to capitalise on impulse purchases at the point of sale.

A repertoire of magazines

When consumers shop for clothes, they tend to have an 'evoked set' – a group of stores which are at the front of their minds. They have a 'repertoire' of shops they visit, with one being their favourite, the one to which they go first. Magazines are

Figure 4.1 Magazines arrayed for sale

no different: consumers need to be satisfied with the content, which means that both advertising and features must be relevant to the reader.

Consumers are not only creatures of habit but they are also quite lazy; they will not waste time going to stores that are not their type of store. In the same way, they will not waste money or time with a magazine that does not suit their style or bank balance.

People are unlikely to read a single magazine. They tend to have a single favourite at any given time but will also buy other magazines, perhaps related to interiors, cookery or gardens, to reflect other interests in their lives. One magazine which neatly encapsulates all these areas is *Grazia*.

The repertoire of magazines changes as the reader goes through various stages of their lives. This can be plotted much like a product lifecycle:

ᗷ children's magazine or comic with simple stories told through pictures
ᗷ pre-teen magazine

- ✑ teenage magazine
- ✑ young adult magazine
- ✑ bridal magazine
- ✑ homes and gardens magazine
- ✑ parent and child magazine
- ✑ family lifestyle magazine
- ✑ hobby magazines.

CASE STUDY: Fashion magazine reader

One young woman talks about how she used magazines as she grew up:

- ✑ 11–13 years old (*Mizz* and *Shout*): As I moved from a child to a 'tween' and began to be interested in appearance, fashion and beauty, I liked the fact that these magazines had hints and tips about topics relevant to my age group. I felt 'educated' by them. Everyone my age was reading these magazines and I was strongly influenced by my peers.
- ✑ 13–14 years old (*Bliss* and *Sugar*): I read *Bliss* more than *Sugar*. I was introduced to *Bliss* by friends of the same age and liked the free gifts and articles. I was educated by some of its articles.
- ✑ 14–15 years old (*Elle Girl* and *Teen Vogue*): It felt as if these magazines were targeted at slightly older girls, which I particularly liked. *Teen Vogue* appealed to my fashion interests and also featured articles and features from young girls around the world. I happened to see *Elle Girl* in a newsagent one day and adored it; I bought it regularly. The fashion and beauty articles were more 'fashion forward' than the more American styling of *Teen Vogue*; it had features on customising clothes, vintage clothes and shops that weren't typical high-street stores. This magazine fed my desire to be more 'individual' than my friends and other girls my age. Instead of shopping at one store, I shopped at many high-street stores, independent boutiques and vintage shops. None of my friends read *Elle Girl*, which made me love it even more. They took it from monthly to 'seasonally' – every three months – and then I couldn't find it any more. Devastating!

(Continued)

- 16–18 years old (*Glamour* and *Elle*): I was much more mature at this stage. Again, these magazines are targeted at older girls which I found appealing. *Glamour* is fun and light-hearted, which I enjoyed, and *Elle* featured more aspirational brands, of which I'd not really heard too much before.
- 21 years old (*Elle*, *Drapers*, *Ideal Home* and *Good Housekeeping*):
  - I still read (and am subscribed to) *Elle*. Occasionally, it has some good articles and the beauty features are brilliant. However, if I wasn't subscribed I wouldn't buy it every month and only if there was someone on the cover I liked! The subscription is cheap, though. I have become tired of *Elle* as it is filled with adverts and I prefer more useful articles! Similarly, I read *Vogue* when starting university (previously, I had read it on and off) but couldn't stand the amount of adverts and found the articles to be 'samey'. However their seasonal 'round-up' reports are good.
  - I read *Drapers* for purposes of my degree study!
  - *Ideal Home* and *Good Housekeeping* are my favourite magazines! They (particularly *Good Housekeeping*) are targeted at a market a lot more mature than me but my degree means that reading fashion magazines purely for pleasure is difficult as I'm analysing everything and it seems as if they are one big advert! Although similar tactics are used in *Good Housekeeping*, it also has interesting and useful articles. I read (and love) *Ideal Home* as I am hoping to buy a house with my partner, so I am looking for ideas and tips!

Looking back, I think it's interesting that when I was beginning to read magazines, I was influenced by my peers and what 'everyone else' was reading. As I began to have a stronger interest in fashion and to mature, I wanted to be more individual than my peers and my choice of magazines reflected this.

Today I am reading magazines that my peers probably don't read and that are targeted at a much older age group. I tend not to read magazines for my target age group or magazines that my friends read. I am more mature for my age than most of my friends and at a more advanced 'life stage', as I am settled with a partner, so this is possibly reflected in my choice of magazines. I'm not sure what this means for my future reading of magazines or what I'll be reading when I'm 25 – *The People's Friend*?

The market for magazines peaks in the 15–24 year age group (Mintel), just as the market for fashion does. This is not surprising given the life stage of this age group; it is the most lucrative market for fashion. Magazines and fashion stores benefit from this group who are predominantly single, looking for a partner and likely to spend their disposable income on clothes and going out.

However, as women are increasingly educated, staying single, childless and in careers for longer, there is a new market which relative newcomer *Grazia* (launched in February 2005) neatly fulfils (see the case study).

CASE STUDY: *Grazia*

In a climate of immediacy and celebrity culture, weekly glossy *Grazia* has picked up many awards and has been described as 'a media icon of our time' that reflects 'society with a fashion fix' and is unique in terms of its presentation and creative treatment.

Grazia's profile (sometimes called a 'media pack'), which is available on its website, explains exactly who they target and how it would be of benefit to a company. The list of their major advertisers reflects almost every upper market brand; their editorial covers the rest.

They say they have the highest loyalty in the glossy magazine market, which makes the magazine effective for building brand awareness. If a brand is featured in editorial and this results in increased sales, the brand may consider advertising in *Grazia*.

The weekly frequency reaches a loyal audience more quickly and with a higher circulation than many of the monthlies combined. It can reach people faster than a monthly such as *Elle*, which could take a publication cycle of 3.5 months. *Grazia*'s profile is not afraid to mention its competitors and emphasise how much more successful *Grazia* is.

With a circulation of 227,100 and a readership of 557,000 (see the next section for the difference between circulation and readership), it is the only weekly glossy with an upper-end market; 77% of the audience is in the

(Continued)

ABC1 social class category and 37% are ABs – an affluent and responsive audience engaging with promotional offers. To quote Jane Bruton, the editor, in October 2005 defending the entry of yet another magazine into an already saturated market:

It's clear we're fulfilling our promise. The shops are telling us so!
Harvey Nichols reported there were long queues to buy an Anne
Klein bag we featured . . . there was an 80% upsurge in sales for
French Connection when we put their top on our Internet section . . .
so to celebrate the fact as Britain's only weekly glossy, we can deliver
fashion right into your hands the day it goes on sale.

—*Grazia.co.uk*

This is a very powerful reason for brands to want to be featured in *Grazia*. Better still, with the online version you can buy without actually making the effort to go to the shops all through *Grazia*'s recommendation.

(Source: www.graziadaily.co.uk)

Women's magazines often include features on menswear because women buy clothing or advise men on style and trends. *Grazia* has recognised this and, rather than go down the route of including menswear in a magazine that its readers consult primarily for their own fashion advice, they launched a trial men's version of *Grazia* called *Gaz7etta*. To date it has yet to come to market.

The magazine–reader relationship – my magazine is my mate?

The relationship between magazine and reader is a bond built on trust, self iden-tity and a number of needs for which the reader turns to magazines – like he or she might turn to a close friend for advice. Consumers take a magazine to their

Table 4.1 Consumer behaviour and magazines

Magazine as a prompt	Consumer behaviour
✤ New season or weather change	✤ Recognition of a need or want
✤ Buy or consult magazines	✤ Search for information
✤ Respond to a feature on how to wear the new trends	✤ Select a number of options
	✤ Visit stores
✤ Identify stores or promotions	✤ Purchase
✤ Reminded of magazine advice by in-store showcards	✤ Post-purchase activities
✤ Confirmation from magazines	

hearts and minds and might describe it as a reflection of themselves, much as they might describe a brand or a trusted friend.

If they did not use magazines for information as a starting point, consumers would spend a lot of time wandering around the high street. Therefore, they might use magazines as a short cut to the high street; new trends are explained in the 'how to wear it' section.

Consider the way consumers make decisions and choices about fashion purchases. If we take traditional consumer behaviour as a starting point, we can relate it to magazines as shown in Table 4.1.

The relationship between readers and magazines has been described by The Henley Centre (2001 and 2004) and discussed by Consterdine (2005) as falling into two distinct and basic categories: information needs and cultural needs.

We consider the informational and cultural needs that magazines fulfil in a fashion context.

Information needs

- ✤ **Instrumental** – it is very important for fashion magazines to deliver information about new retailers or brands and new trends so that readers are 'in the know'.
- ✤ **Analysis** – fashion magazines do not necessarily consider world issues, ethical issues, the role of women in society and cultural issues in the same depth

as a broadsheet newspaper but it is enough to keep the fashion consumer aware of current affairs.

✥ **Enlightenment** – in a fashion magazine, articles on cinema, books and art exhibitions tend to fall into the cultural area of 'rom-coms', 'chick lit' and art installations reflecting fashion e.g. the costumes were the draw in the Supremes exhibition.

✥ **Self-enhancement** – fashion magazines include information on diet and beauty regimes and skills acquisition e.g. cookery and craft features. Aspirational information can include the latest type of yoga the stars are embracing.

Consumers may feel that they are informed by magazines and that they can discuss, for example, the latest exhibition because magazines have given them the basics, although they may not have taken time to visit the exhibition.

Cultural needs

✥ **Ritual** – readers find satisfaction in buying *Grazia* every week and *Vogue* every month or in buying a selection of magazines before boarding a train or plane.

✥ **Default** – readers glance at magazines when waiting in the doctor's surgery or at a friend's house. *Grazia* often publishes letters which say that a new 'convert' picked it up 'by mistake' but that it is now a weekly staple. Readers may not necessarily believe that this is an actual letter but it may be an amalgamation of a number of letters.

✥ **Relaxation** – flicking through glossy magazines is a method of relaxing. Where and when readers do this is also a key feature of the relationship with a magazine. There is a physical element and relationship with a magazine: to date, it is not possible to look at a magazine online whilst in the bath.

✥ **Entertainment** – amusement is provided in terms of funny stories, puzzles and quizzes, or pictures of celebrities in bizarre outfits.

✥ **Escapism** – stories describe different lives, such as those of celebrities, or features of designer homes.

The Henley Centre also concluded that magazines engage with readers on a very personal level in four main ways: trust, support, status and participation. We consider each of these areas with fashion as a focus.

Trust

Readers have a close relationship with the magazine that they buy most often and the magazine can be seen as a trusted source of information. Most fashion magazines build on this notion of trust by delivering a combination of articles and fashion features which match the reader's needs; it becomes a trusted friend.

Support

Magazines reflect and support readers through the phases of their lives. Fashion and lifestyle magazines aimed at women who are of childbearing age have features on managing the balance between family and work life, clothes for returning to work, advice on returning to work, diet and exercise regimes, décor for kids' bedrooms, storage ideas, child-friendly holiday destinations and holiday wardrobe staples. Readers might consult them, like a friend, in a time of change or crisis.

Status

If anything confers status and self esteem, then clothing choices do for the fashion-conscious consumer. The magazine that gives the consumer this information also acts as a status-enhancing choice. The choice of magazine is a reflection of oneself. Compare two women next time you are on public transport: one reading *Vogue* and one reading one of the gossip weeklies; how do these women differ?

Participation

By choosing a certain magazine, readers are participating in a community of readers who support charities, write e-mails and letters, join websites and read online blogs. Most magazines now have an online version of the magazine; it is not a substitute for the glossy magazine but a valuable addition: for the consumer, it gives daily updates direct to the inbox, like a friend; for the magazine, the main benefit is that it reminds the reader of the magazine brand. It can become a two-way conversation on a blog or Facebook. Pressing the 'Like' button gives readers an opportunity to participate and gives magazines valuable feedback.

Teenage magazines

Magazines aimed at teenagers are almost a specialist area of their own but deserve a mention here as they can be part of a family of brands. They hope to capture the loyalty of their consumers and then move them on through the other magazines in the stable as their lifestyle moves on. An example of this is *Teen Vogue* from the Condé Nast group.

Teenagers' needs are somewhat different to the more mature consumer of magazines. Teen magazines are perhaps even more trusted than maturer publications as this is a time in teens' lives when how they look is of paramount importance. The subject matter is specifically targeted to answer their needs in, for example, sexual matters (rather than asking adults or relying on friends, they trust a magazine for information). Beauty and body issues are an important part of such magazines.

Editors of teen magazines take their responsibilities very seriously and have what can only be described as a 'rolling calendar' of the issues that all teenagers confront on an annual basis.

Advertising costs, circulation and context

A strong bond between consumers and their chosen brand of magazine delivers trust in the magazine content, including the advertising. Because consumers use magazines as an authoritative source of fashion information, it can be suggested that they do not view the advertising as intrusive (unlike in other media channels, such as television).

Indeed, advertising is integral to the enjoyment of magazines and is seen as part of the entertainment, not least because readers have paid to allow this content into their lives. They choose the magazine and all that is in it by paying; they give magazines permission to advertise brands which they are likely to own or which they aspire to own in the future.

The cost of advertising in a magazine is strongly related to the position of the advertisement within the magazine (the context) and the magazine's circulation (the number of copies sold). Advertising costs are available from companies and are known as the 'rate card'. The higher the circulation of a magazine, the higher the cost of advertising as there are more opportunities for people to see the advert. Opportunities-to-see figures (sometimes known as OTS figures) are directly related to circulation figures but this might be a simplistic way of measuring the number of times a reader is exposed to an advert.

Circulation figures for most magazines are readily available on the Internet. However, because people revisit magazines and pass them on to friends, it has been estimated that a magazine is read 2.5 times. It can be suggested that the circulation figures do not necessarily reflect accurately how many times an advert may be seen.

Whilst the costs of advertising are listed and readily available, they are not necessarily exact as there can be negotiation with an advertiser if a long contract is desired. Magazines are also open to advertising cost negotiation at times when circulation may fall; holiday periods demonstrate significant dips in copies sold. Direct subscriptions are therefore an important strategy for magazines; they sign readers up for a whole year by offering significant savings and free gifts.

As a general rule, the most expensive page in a magazine is the outside back cover (OBC). People carry a magazine by rolling it inwards to protect the cover and, therefore, the back cover is always on view, which is like a moving advert exposed to a number of audiences.

In general, after the back page, the most expensive positions are (in descending order):

- **the first double-page spread** (FDPS) or **inside the front cover** (IFC) – the first thing to which a reader is exposed
- **the first fifth** (20%) where interest level is at its highest
- **the first third** (33%) commands the next highest price.

A right-hand page (RHP) can add 5% to the cost, as our eye movement is left to right. The closer to an important feature or story, the more expensive the advertising.

The final quarter or third of the magazine is less expensive to advertise in because it is where we are beginning to lose interest. However, magazine readers have been observed flicking through from the back when they return to peruse a magazine for a second time. This supports the cost of the back page being highest but is not reflected in other adverts near the back. This may mean that advertising costs do not necessarily reflect reader behaviour.

The most interesting point to note in a rate card is the cost of an advertorial: this can add 40% to the cost of any position in the magazine as it is like a testimonial written by an influential journalist. To some readers, it is not immediately apparent that it is an advert. The word 'promotion' or 'advertorial' often appears in an unobtrusive position and font size.

Product placement

Fashion product placement in editorial and advertorial is perhaps even more trusted when readers have a relationship with a magazine. A buyer in a company purchases products to match their target market (rather than products they particularly like); in the same way, a magazine features garments that match the readership.

Magazines feature how to get the look, new products to solve readers' beauty crises, menus to make in minutes and interior styling features. All of these features will match the target market of the magazine. It appears that an editor has taken time out to introduce the readers to products that enhance their lives. Because they trust the magazine, readers do not see it as part of a publicity machine. To the untrained eye, it seems benevolent.

Because of this, fashion public relations (PR) agents spend much of their time in attempting to get products placed in magazines for free. The position and size of the placement is calculated by the PR function or an external agency, such as Dunnings.

Advertising value equivalent (AVE)

Because the cost of advertising is calculated by circulation and context, the same figures can be used by companies to calculate how much the placement would have cost if it had been an actual advert. This is known as 'advertising value equivalent' (AVE) or 'rate card value' (RCV).

The company can look at the position and context in which product placement has been achieved and calculate how much of the page has been taken up by the product placement. The page is divided into quarters and the cost of a whole page of advertising is divided by four.

This gives companies a simple value for their coverage; however there are a number of variables that companies could and should build into this calculation:

- **Front cover placement:** no-one can advertise on the front cover of a magazine but because the front cover sells magazines this is a much more valuable variable – a Kate Moss, Kate Middleton or Victoria Beckham cover can lift sales by a third.
- **Position in the magazine:** the first third is highly desirable for a brand.
- **Position on the page:** the centre or top right of the page may be more valuable than the bottom left.
- **The size of the image compared with others on the page** (the larger the image, the more valuable).
- **The prestige of the media channel** – being featured in the highest circulation glossy magazines is the aim of every fashion brand.

The editorial fashion spread in Figure 4.2 brings a diverse range of black and white merchandise together under a 'theme'. This product placement was in the first 20% of the magazine.

The credibility of product placement in a magazine should not be understated. It has been said that it increases the 'value' by 2.5 times. A whole page dedicated to a product is the most valuable product placement a company could have – it is worth 2.5 times more than it would have cost as an advert, and all without the costs of actually producing an advert.

The relationship between advertising and product placement

In the film *The Devil wears Prada*, when viewing the clothes in preparation for a fashion shoot, the editor asks 'Where are our sponsors?' (The Americans call their advertisers 'sponsors'.) This is an important issue for magazines.

Magazines do not make nearly enough money from the cover price to pay for the salaries, celebrity photographs, investigative reports, location shoot costs, photographers, hair and beauty stylists, and so on, that every issue requires. (The fees for celebrity photographers, such as Mario Testino and Patrick Demarchelier, are very high.) The cover price of a magazine is heavily subsidised by advertising revenues; magazines could not survive without advertisers. Therefore, it is not surprising that advertisers get some editorial coverage 'in return'. This is a symbiotic relationship which should not be underestimated.

Figure 4.2 *Grazia* concentrates on a monochrome theme

Advertising campaigns seldom appear in isolation; they are normally sup-ported by a PR campaign that includes other tools of promotion. In a single issue of a magazine, there is a careful balance between advertising and edito-rial so as not to make the practice overt to the reader. However, these are long-term relationships and if a brand only advertises in alternate months, it is highly likely that it will achieve some product placement in the intervening issues.

Francesca Burns, a stylist at *Vogue* comments (Zarrella 2012):

---

at *i-D* you didn't necessarily have to shoot all your advertisers but *Vogue* is big business and there are a lot of boxes to tick.

—*The Business of Fashion, 1 April 2012*

This would seem to confirm the relationship between advertising revenue and editorial content.

Monthly and weekly magazines

Monthly and weekly magazines do not compete with each other – they are used in different ways.

With the growth of the consumer's response to and appetite for fast fashion, it is probably not surprising that circulation figures (even when aggregated) for weekly magazines are higher than circulation figures monthlies, with their longer lead times.

Weeklies fill a niche in offering immediacy and monthlies are more suited to building brand awareness and long-term trends. However, monthlies have had to play catch up in the age of social media.

Weeklies inform the reader about the fashions of the moment, being more of a fashion shopping guide or prompt, and have fewer adverts which are image led. Their adverts are product led in contrast to monthlies, which have more space not only for adverts built on image but also for features about fashion leaders and catwalk collections for next season. Monthly magazines are aimed at the more fashion-forward consumer and tend to be kept for longer, almost as a reference.

In weekly magazines, women find advice on how to wear the look now; monthlies are for women who are more confident and can take an image, a theme, a mood or a style and interpret it for themselves without a fashion dictat. *Vogue* is much more 'fashion forward' than a weekly like *Grazia*, which shows trends that are available to buy now (see Figure 4.2).

Most monthly and weekly magazines have a parallel online magazine, offering daily snippets of news and style updates. They provide a virtual reminder of the magazine between issues. To date, these daily updates are free.

Weekend supplements

Newspaper circulation is on a downward curve but weekend newspapers that include style supplements are showing some growth. This reflects the consumer who has more time to read newspapers at the weekend (including fashion and lifestyle supplements) as daily news is disseminated by radio, TV and, increasingly, the Internet. These supplements are the same as traditional magazines – they reflect the interests of the target market.

There is a difference between the *Financial Times* 'how to spend it' supplement and the tabloids' supplements. Although these are newspaper supplements, they share some of the characteristics of traditional magazines in that they tend to be glossy and are kept longer than the newspaper.

Celebrity and gossip magazines

Celebrity and gossip magazines have been the most successful types of magazine, in terms of circulation growth, in recent years. Reflecting a cultural obsession with celebrity and the minutiae of their lives (see Chapter 6), these magazines have an enormous market share. Fashion stories are mixed with celebrity stories.

Advertising in celebrity magazines is aimed at the target market; readers do not necessarily have the level of fashion consciousness of typical *Vogue* readers, but they are still fashion conscious. Many up-market brands do not let celebrity and gossip magazines use their clothes in fashion editorial. The top brands tend to be shown on a red carpet with a celebrity wearing them, rather than in an overt advert or a product placement.

The recession and magazine advertising

It is worth noting that, during an economic recession, advertising is often one of the first budgets to be cut. There are a number of reasons for this, not least that it is extremely difficult for companies to evaluate the effectiveness of advertising. However, during previous recessions (in the late 1980s and early to mid 1990s), one area of the fashion communications business has always thrived and grown: this is PR.

Companies are aware of the value of product placement and look to this to keep their brand in the public domain during a recession when they may not be using traditional advertising.

Summary

This chapter has discussed the role fashion magazines play in consumers' lives, from a behavioural and usage perspective. It has explored the cost of magazine advertising and the cover price revenue. The value of product placement and its relationship with advertising has been elucidated.

Chapter 8 covers trade press magazines.

References

Consterdine, G. (2005) 'How magazine adverting works', available at www.consterdine.com/articlefiles/42/HMAW5.pdf [Accessed 26 May 2011].

Henley Centre (2001) 'Redwood Engagement Survey'.

Henley Centre (2004) 'Planning for Consumer Change'.

Mintel (2010) *Media and Fashion UK*.

PPA, www.ppa.co.uk/ppa-marketing [Accessed 26 May 2011].

The Devil Wears Prada, film (2006) directed by David Frankel. Fox 2000 Pictures, USA.

Zarrella, K. K. (2012) 'The Creative Class: Francesca Burns', available at www.businessoffashion.com/2012/04/the-creative-class-francesca-burns.html#more-30625 [Accessed 1 May 2012].

Activities

1 Visit a newsagent or store selling magazines and observe or measure the space that magazines take up. Compare women's fashion magazines with men's fashion magazines.

2 Look at the position in a shop of the most popular magazines and investigate their circulation figures.

3 Select a magazine and identify the information and cultural needs that it satisfies.

4 Compare and contrast magazines for different market segments.

5 Add up the advertising revenue from a magazine using their rate card.

6 Select a magazine to follow over a period of time. You will need to look at a minimum of four issues to see a pattern emerging.
   a List the advertising the magazine carries.
   b Find the same companies being featured in editorials.

7 Measure the page space given to product placement in a magazine where the same company takes advertising space.

8 Work out the AVE of some product placements; add in some descriptions of the variables which may make it even more valuable.

9 Compare the content and tone of men's and women's magazines.

10 Look at newspaper supplements to see which aspects they share with traditional magazines and which aspects set them apart.

5

THE ROLE OF PUBLIC RELATIONS

Don't pay any attention to what they write about you. Just measure it in inches.

—Andy Warhol, www.warholfoundation.org

THIS CHAPTER:

- ⤷ defines public relations

- ⤷ explains how public relations supports fashion communication strategies

- ⤷ describes the difference between in-house public relations departments and public relations agencies

- ⤷ discusses measuring the value and effectiveness of public relations.

Introduction

Public relations (PR) is defined by the Institute of Public Relations as the 'planned and sustained effort to establish and maintain goodwill and understanding between an organisation and its publics'. As a generic definition of PR, this is acceptable and would cover a lot of bases in most organisations. However, the role of PR for a fashion company is often somewhat different.

Who carries out the PR function?

Some organisations have public relations departments or the function can be undertaken by an outside agency. Sometimes companies use a combination of both. The people who undertake public relations activities are often called 'public relations agents', abbreviated to PR, so 'PR' can mean a department or a person undertaking the function.

The case study gives a job advertisement for a PR assistant in a firm that produces beauty products.

CASE STUDY: Job advertisement for a PR assistant

Job Title

PR Assistant across three brands: St. Tropez, Charles Worthington and Sanctuary Spa.

Brand History

PZ Cussons has recently formed an exciting new division in the beauty world. St. Tropez, Charles Worthington and Sanctuary Spa have now combined to form PZ Cussons Beauty. This is a new role and a key entry-level position for anyone interested in PR and the beauty industry.

Job Specification

The candidate will be expected to be enthusiastic, motivated and extremely hard working. A high level of passion for PR is essential. Ideally the candidate

(Continued)

will be well presented, both in fashion and beauty. A knowledge of global cosmetic, fashion, music and media trends are key for this role.

Tasks will include:

- ✎ scanning the media, formatting press coverage and distributing to wider teams internally
- ✎ booking VIP treatments for journalists, media and celebrities and liaising with artist relation teams, including VIP tanning experts
- ✎ assisting at events including The Prince's Trust Ball, various London Fashion Week shows, new product launches and music festivals
- ✎ trialling new products and assisting in brainstorming with product development teams for innovation
- ✎ working with celebrity facialists, session stylists and beauty therapists
- ✎ assisting in copy reading for press releases and advertorials
- ✎ monitoring stock levels and deliveries of PR stock – for London office or external events
- ✎ liaising with other departments including sales, product development, online marketing, salon marketing and retail marketing to ensure that each brand message is constant.

Salary

Negotiable depending upon previous experience but consistent with the industry standard.

The main purpose in fashion of public relations personnel is to ensure that 'hero' products (the main fashion trend products of the season), or brands, retailers and companies are reflected in a positive light by being placed in the public domain via the media (such as magazines, films and TV). As we saw in Chapter 4, magazines are one of the most important and trusted media vehicles for fashion companies to reach their target market. Apart from traditional advertising, magazines have a number of pages dedicated to editorial features and these offer enormous opportunities to place and promote the company and the product for no direct cost. Product placements are not the traditional paid-for or sponsored adverts but are 'disguised' as editorial content that features the best beauty products, the little black dress, or how to get the catwalk trends on the high street.

The costs of PR

It costs money for a company to support a PR function but there is no direct cost to the brand for an image being shown in the media as part of a fashion story. In contrast, a magazine may pay to show a visual from a catwalk show.

Public relations has had some negative associations – it can be regarded as 'spin'. On occasions, it may be used to deflect poor press coverage but, in general, PR in fashion is about promoting and placing the product in the media and in the public domain via magazines, TV, films, online (social media, blogging and pinterest) and so on.

Magazines do not gain their revenue from the cover price but from the advertising that is placed in them (see Chapter 4). The cost of advertising depends on the position in the magazine and varies between publications but, in essence, it is a high cost to a brand.

PR plays a supporting role to advertising. For companies that do not have an advertising budget or campaign, PR may be their only way of getting a product into the public arena. This can be particularly important during a recession.

The other costs of PR include the retention of an agency or an in-house PR function (sometimes called the 'press office'), the costs of hospitality for journalists and the cost of 'gifting' products.

The role of the journalist in PR

Journalists are constantly looking for stories and features. They have deadlines. Many are freelance. They have their media to sell. Journalists are therefore extremely important people in the relationship between a PR function and the media. For a PR agent, cultivating and maintaining relationships with contacts in the media is vital.

Much like consumers, journalists are bombarded by messages. It is important to be seen to be different. A journalist will be contacted by many PR agents; it is important, therefore, for a PR agent to know where the journalists' interests lie, what they are working on, and what is coming up in future issues. Informal meetings can encourage this interaction. One PR agency invites journalists for breakfast meetings; croissants and coffee are served in a relatively informal environment on the way to the office. This maintains contact and is low key rather than a pressured approach. If you make and maintain contact, journalists come to rely on you as a good source and will give you coverage.

It has been said that journalists are a necessary evil. Journalists would probably say the same about their PR contacts. Whatever the truth of this, there is a symbiotic relationship – both parties need and use each other.

There are some very influential media, journalists, editors, fashion stylists, models, bloggers and celebrities, including *Vogue*, Hilary Alexander, Suzy Menkes, Katie Grand, Garance Doré, Anna Wintour, Alexandra Schulman, Kate Moss and Victoria Beckham.

Credibility

The credibility factor of PR or product placement should not be underestimated.

PR is an extremely useful tool to generate positive media coverage. Consumers are very aware of traditional, paid-for advertising but PR is more subtle. To the untrained eye, a journalist, blogger, celebrity or stylist may appear to be endorsing a product. It is a credible and believable way of reaching the consumer especially in today's noisy, crowded and cluttered media environment.

How PR differs from traditional advertising

In magazines, traditional advertising features are normally full page and placed at regular intervals throughout the magazine with a clear source of origin (see Chapter 4).

In contrast, PR features can come under a number of guises and appear to be stories or features on topics such as:

- new trends
- little black dresses
- chic on the cheap, sometimes called 'minted or skinted' or 'get the look for less'
- your capsule holiday wardrobe
- a fashion, arts or sporting sponsorship event.

Magazines have regular features that are part of the fashion season cycle. Almost every week or month there will be a variation on these themes, for example:

- ↯ **Autumn/Winter:** Trends are illustrated as the catwalk shows are airing. This coverage may support PR pages on how to pick up on the trend in the high street at a more reasonable price. *Vogue's* biggest issue is in September to support the new collections.
- ↯ **Christmas:** This season may be supported by a PR feature focussing on red garments, gifts and accessories. There will be features on 'Gifts for Girls', 'Gifts for Him' and 'Gifts for people who have everything'.
- ↯ **Spring/Summer:** Features may describe how to wear the new colour palette and there may be a PR section on accessories. It may also be supported by a beauty section about cosmetics or on how to get a 'bikini body'.

Journalists are inventive in extending these themes throughout the year. It is important for a PR company to find out what may be the subject of a future feature and ensure that they can contribute one of their brands.

Fashion editors know what the main fashion feature will be for any month or week. Some issues, such as a Christmas one, will be planned 4–6 months ahead. Right up to the publication deadline, journalists will be inserting relevant features. The issues that coincide with international fashion weeks across the cities of the world will have a fairly set list of contents. For example, if a designer shows a monochrome palette, the magazine may 'call up' (ring or e-mail PR departments or companies to request) garment samples or visual images from their contacts at three levels of the market and feature a black and white top, jewellery, shoes and belts to demonstrate to the consumer how to translate the trend into a more mainstream wardrobe. One extreme (and normally expensive) designer garment or accessory is a focal point (the 'hero' garment that provides inspiration) from which more affordable and wearable options radiate.

How PR supports traditional advertising

It is no mere coincidence that the fashion companies who pay for traditional advertising in a magazine also get some PR coverage within the same issue or perhaps on alternate weeks or months.

PR and product placement serve to:

- remind customers of the brand
- recall previous advertising to the customer's mind
- promote recognition of the brand 'handwriting' (i.e. the brand's image)
- reinforce the fashion credentials of the brand.

PR with no advertising budget

New or small, edgy and independent brands often do not have an advertising budget and PR is their way to generate coverage.

Magazines are an opportunity to showcase new brands. When they have a bigger profile in the future, the magazine that showcased the brand normally gets the advertising revenue.

PR companies are also responsible for arranging and submitting celebrity pictures and stories to support magazine features.

PR as an 'afterthought'

For a long time, PR was seen as the poor relation of advertising. There is now a better understanding of how PR supports and adds credibility to traditional advertising and that it is more influential with a more savvy consumer who does not necessarily respond to overt promotional tools. PR has become a covert channel which has gained momentum in recent years. PR has become established as a valuable tool in its own right instead of as an 'add on'.

In traditional advertising, communication about the products to be featured is an important part of the brief because, inevitably, advertising will stimulate demand. A close liaison with the buying and distribution teams will be necessary. However, even with all the planning in the world, advertising may stimulate more demand than can be fulfilled. This was the case with Gap, which promoted a striped scarf in its Christmas advertising. In PR activity, it was picked up as being at a reasonable price as a 'stocking filler'; it immediately sold out and repeat stock could not be guaranteed for Christmas. Indeed, the extra stock was sitting in markdown as Gap moved on to the Spring–Summer season because Christmas had been and gone by the time the repeat delivery arrived. Forecasting demand has never been an exact science and adding a prominent and credible product placement into the equation can be as damaging as understimulation of demand. Because PR is a more credible source of communication than advertising, it can create great demand. It is extremely important that featured merchandise is available to purchase, to prevent customer disappointment. Fast fashion is particularly prone to customer disappointment (Barnes and Lea-Greenwood, 2010). Placement often includes a slogan, such as 'get it before it goes', to remind customers of the exclusive or narrow distribution strategy.

How gender affects PR

Women are generally confident, browsing customers. Men, however, have been described by Mintel as 'hit-and-run' or 'hunter–gatherer' shoppers. PR plays a very important role in the media when it comes to the male consumer of fashion. As they shop in a different way to women, they do not need to see a number of different ideas.

Much as with gadgets, fashion can be shown to men in shop windows and magazines and they will act upon 'advice'. In general, men's magazines do not have as much visual product placement as women's; however the PR information will be embedded in an editorial rather more subtly.

Working out the value of product placement

PR personnel attempt to value how much a product placement would have cost if it was a traditional advertisement. They use the following terms interchangeably:

- advertising value equivalent (AVE)
- rate card value (RCV)

A key issue in valuing a product placement is that editorial treatment is said to be worth three to four times a traditional piece of advertising.

To be even more precise in valuing a piece of PR or product placement, it is useful to add into the calculation the importance of the placement based on its size, what is around it, nearby and opposite. These important details (variables) will change within and between publications.

The following variables all affect the value of product placement:

- facing matter
- position in the publication
- number of times mentioned or shown in the film or TV programme
- size of image
- position on the page
- circulation, box-office or TV viewing figures.

From 1 March 2011, the UK has allowed product placement in television programmes.

For anyone who has observed product placement on overseas TV channels, which can be quite overt, it will be interesting to watch how it is used in the relatively conservative TV environment of the UK.

Types of PR function

PR agencies

PR agencies normally operate from a showroom that houses a 'capsule range' for each client. These are the hero pieces of the season, which are likely to be picked for fashion features. These showrooms tend to be in the heart of the city to make visits and sample call-ups accessible to journalists working nearby or within cheap courier distance. During the recession, interns walk to magazine offices.

External PR agencies will have a number of clients, not all fashion companies. The major advantage of this is that the agency will have a wide range of contacts and experience across different types of media. The disadvantage is that they have to spread their effort over a number of different brands.

For a retainer fee (the size of which is a closely guarded secret in the industry), an agency will endeavour to keep the brand or retailer in the media arena, in maga-zines, television programmes and films that address the target market. When needed, an agency manages events, such as sponsoring an art exhibition, on behalf of the brand. The agency may also organise press days, when journalists are invited to view new collections and are given 'look books' (magazines that show the key trends in a collection) that can be used as a resource when they are planning future stories.

External agencies tend to be extremely rigorous in collating and measuring press coverage. Some agencies call themselves 'full-service agencies'. However, there is some discussion as to how full their services are: they do not tend to include advertising (such as an advertising agency would).

In-house PR departments

Some brands or retailers operate their PR function from within the organisation. It is sometimes called a 'press office', which means that they respond to press queries but are less than proactive. The main advantage of this is that the PR team only have a single brand to look after and tend to have a good understanding of the brand and its history. They are close to the brand physically and psychically. They can avoid some of the problems associated with the demand that PR stimulates, by liaising with the buying and merchandising function, which are normally in the same location. The costs of an in-house PR function are not as obvious as they would be if they were being generated by an agency.

The disadvantage is that the in-house team may not have as much experience and breadth of contacts. It may not work as effectively as it could on behalf of the company, as the threat of losing the business is not as intense. A number of high-profile fashion companies have outsourced their PR function for these reasons.

In-house PR functions do not tend to be as rigorous in their collection and evaluation of coverage as external agencies.

The role of the PR function

Contacts

As is often said, it's not about what you know but who you know. Media agencies can provide databases of journalists but many fashion PR agents have their own list of contacts with whom they have built up long-term relationships. They understand the needs of the magazine and the target market rather than using a 'scatter-gun' approach in which they contact a variety of publications.

Press releases

If contacts in the media are the lifeblood of the PR industry, then the press release is the major organ.

There are a number of useful websites that attempt to define how to write a press release but most agencies have their own in-house style. The main issues are to ensure that the press release is grammatically and factually correct as journalists will copy and paste a press release into a feature.

If a press release is time sensitive, there may be an 'embargo' date. This is a date on which the information can be released to the public.

A press release will normally be circulated:

- ♮ at the beginning of the season
- ♮ mid season
- ♮ at the end of the season
- ♮ to announce any news on an ad-hoc basis (see Figure. 5.1).

A press release can vary from a one-page update to a larger document with images. Tonia Bastyan produces a complete magazine that she issues to the press (see Figure 5.2).

Show cards

Show cards support the publicity which has been achieved. They may show pictures of the PR generated on a swing ticket attached to the garment or hanger which says 'As seen in' or 'As featured in' a specific magazine. They can be a useful prompt to customers during their purchasing activity: they confirm that the garment has been 'selected' by the fashion media and is therefore covetable.

Sponsorship

The PR function will be involved in managing any sponsorships or collaborations in which a company becomes involved. The PR function organises the sponsorship or event, manages the relationship, tracks the coverage in the media and gives feedback.

Sponsorship can be of events, sports or music personalities and may be long- or short-term. It is very important that there is a fit between the brand and the

PRESS RELEASE

Label breaks the rules with Kate Moss for Rimmel

London, August 2003: Funky beauty products manufacturer, Rimmel, is featuring Kate Moss as you have never seen her before in a bid to launch its new advertising campaign for Extreme Definition comb mascara. The 30 second film, 'Rebellious', which breaks on September 5th, is the latest work from agency Label, the fashion and lifestyle division of J. Walter Thompson.

Label's latest work in the Rimmel London campaign sees Kate Moss breaking the rules and generally causing anarchy in a traditional palace setting: tearing down curtains, spraying champagne, swinging from a chandelier and teasing a palace guard.

Working with top fashion photographer-turned director Sean Ellis, the agency wanted to have Kate's personality shine through, to capture her punk princess spirit and rebelliousness that goes with the revolutionary nature of the product.

"The key to capturing Kate's naturally playful and rebellious side was to get her to relax and just really enjoy herself on set, sometimes unaware that the camera was even rolling" said Kenny Hill, Account Director at Label.

Coty hopes that the launch of the new comb mascara will be a runaway success and help to extend Rimmel's No.1 status in the UK colour cosmetics market. The campaign will also be used to launch the product globally from Germany to the USA, where Rimmel is one of the fastest growing cosmetic brands and the most successful new brand launch in retail giant WalMart.

The TV campaign will break on September 5th, followed by interactive work on Sky which will build on Rimmel's previous successful interactive work with the channel. Print support will run in women's and style press, also featuring Kate Moss in work shot for Label by Craig McDean.

The Rimmel London campaign continues to build on the brand's edgy, experimental personality and set Rimmel apart from its competitors. According to Kenny Hill "Girls fed up with the over-retouched and unattainable visions of 'perfect' beauty peddled by much of the beauty industry. With Kate Moss and the London theme we strive to produce work for Rimmel that is an antidote for that cynicism".

The campaign was written and art directed by Robin Harvey, Blaise Douglas and Richard Midgley and directed by Sean Ellis through RSA.
Media planning/buying through OMD.

For more information contact Kenny Hill, Account Manager at JWT on ▮▮▮▮▮▮▮▮ or Chrissie Barker, Communications Director at JWT on ▮▮▮▮▮▮▮.

Figure 5.1 Rimmel press release

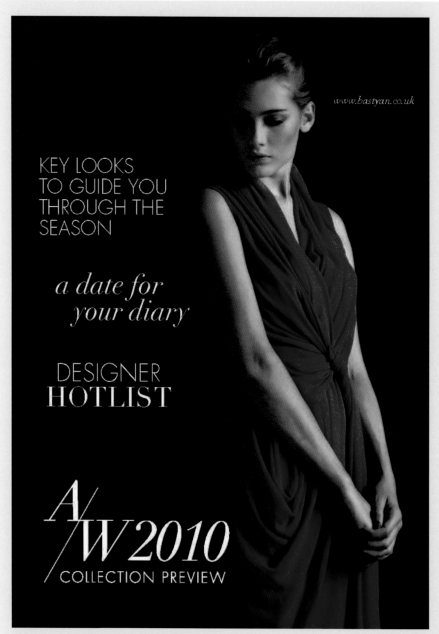

Figure 5.2 Bastyan press magazine

event or person. For example, River Island has sponsored Graduate Fashion Week, Cartier has sponsored Polo and Nike has sponsored Tiger Woods in long-term sponsorships. Nick Faldo, the golfer, was for many years sponsored by Pringle, but when his game faded and Pringle repositioned as a more fashion-orientated brand, it was time for them to part company.

Sponsorship and celebrity endorsements can sometimes be very similar arrangements. At first, sponsorship of a band may simply involve dressing the musicians. As the fan base grows, the band members may turn into celebrity endorsers or even collaborate on collections. Some celebrities are accidental ambassadors for the brand at first. Paul Weller (for Ben Sherman) and Amy Winehouse (for Fred Perry) became involved in designing special-edition collections for the brands they liked to wear. This gives the brand a high credibility factor.

Events management

Events are part of the PR remit. Even if a specific events management company is employed, it is important that the PR people know what is involved, in order to manage the process.

The types of event that fashion and PR companies organise can include:

- fashion shows
- pop-up stores
- new store openings
- press days
- product launches
- charity events.

The objectives of an event will inform the strategy and they should always be kept in mind. An event is part information and part entertainment. Events generate goodwill amongst the public and the press. You should keep in mind the following questions:

- **Point** – what are the objectives?
- **People** – who should be invited?
- **Process** – what needs to be organised?
- **Post-event activities** – how will the coverage be followed up?

If we take the example of organising a fashion show, which many students like to do, it is important to have a plan of activities working backwards from the date of the show. It is known as a 'critical path' and shows the actions that have to be undertaken. Such a plan shows that there are a lot of organisational issues, which may include:

- deciding on a theme
- booking the venue
- hiring a catwalk, stage and chairs
- linking up with a charity
- ordering and filling goody bags
- arranging models, makeup, music and choreography
- arranging refreshments and front of house staff
- printing and distributing invitations and publicity
- carry out a health and safety risk assessment.

Providing evidence of effectiveness

An important part of the role of the PR function is to provide feedback to the client (or the company) proving that an increase in sales or interest has been generated. There are external agencies that collate and evaluate media coverage. These agencies have a number of names:

- press cuttings agency
- clippings agency
- media intelligence
- media monitoring.

In essence, they all do the same thing: they collate coverage in any medium to ensure that the PR company does not miss any coverage. This allows the PR function to utilise its time in gaining coverage, rather than checking for it. The two most well-known agencies are Cision and Durrants. A challenge for companies with global representation is how the brand is communicated in overseas markets; a company such as Cision has an international network of partners monitoring PR coverage across the world.

The agencies can also collate competitor coverage if required. Companies charge a daily fee for reading (researching) and then a fee for each piece of coverage that they forward to the brand or PR agency in hard copy or electronic form.

It has been noted, during discussions with PR personnel, that this method of communicating results does not always make full use of calculating the advertising value equivalent (AVE). Few of the variables, such as the profile of the publication, the position of the PR feature in the whole publication and the position on the page, are factored in. This is an area that agencies and in-house PR could work out relatively easily and use to make an even more robust case for their efforts.

The Association for Measurement and Evaluation of Communications (AMEC) has been involved in raising the profile of PR for a number of years. It suggests that the sole use of and over-reliance upon simple AVEs as a method of evaluation has become outdated.

A PR company clearly displayed to a client a clippings file for a month's coverage. A lot of coverage had been generated in a variety of media and the clippings agency presented the visual evidence in an attractive format for the client. However, on closer inspection and questioning, the client discovered that the analysis did not include factors such as the following:

- the gravitas of the publication
- the position in the publication
- the circulation figures
- the seniority and expertise of the journalist.

Figure 5.3 shows an example of a clippings file.

Crisis management

Because the fashion industry is about image, protecting the image of a brand can be an important part of the PR remit. The fashion industry has more opportunity than most industries to shock (issues surrounding nudism and size zero models, for example). It is open to criticism for its sourcing policies as much of the manufacturing is done in countries with low labour costs.

There have been many instances of the media revealing poor practices in the fashion industry. PR departments are often expected to defend companies against

Figure 5.3 A clippings file

charges of poor practices and make a positive response to them. A PR department is the spokesperson on behalf of the brand. It attempts to explain:

- ✑ how factories are audited
- ✑ how subcontracting may have occurred without the company's knowledge
- ✑ what the company has done about the revelations
- ✑ what future strategies are being brought into operation.

In this way, the PR function attempts to educate and inform the public. However, as this chapter has demonstrated and from research conducted in PR companies, fashion PR tends to concern itself with product placement rather than crisis management.

Summary

This chapter has shown how important the PR function is in the fashion industry. It has explained the costs and functions of PR.

References

Association for Measurement and Evaluation of Communications (AMEC), www.amecorg .com [Accessed 13 December 2011].

Barnes, E. and Lea-Greenwood, G. (2010) 'Fast fashion in the retail store environment', *International Journal of Retail & Distribution Management*, 38(10):760–772.

Cision, uk.Cision.com [Accessed 23 June 2011].

Durrants, www.Durrants.co.uk [Accessed 23 June 2011].

Activities

1. Identify a garment in a piece of PR (not advertising) in a magazine (or other form of media). Posing as a genuine customer, visit the store (or telephone or visit the website) to explore the availability of the product, its position and promotion in the store environment, the reaction of staff to a request and so on. What comments can you make about product availability and communication within the company and with the PR function?

2. Work out the advertising value equivalent (AVE) for some different types of media, for example magazines, TV programmes and the cinema. Access rate cards and circulation and viewing figures to gather data. Calculate a simple AVE and then add in some variables suggested in this chapter.

3. Compare and contrast the PR coverage between women's and men's magazines. In what way is the PR coverage different? Is it more or less subtle in magazines and media targeted at men than in those targeted at women?

4. Carry out a content analysis of a magazine of your choice. Count the pages of traditional advertising and the PR pages. Make any links you can between the advertising and PR pages. This may need to be over a period of time.

5   Identify a brand that needs PR coverage and write a press release. Think about which publications you might target and how you would go about this.

6   Plan a fashion show.

7   Identify a brand which has received some negative publicity and write a press release which defends the brand's position and accentuates its positive features.

8   Analyse a sponsorship or collaboration and discuss the relevance and 'fit' with the brand.

Discussion questions

I   To what extent do you think the average consumer of media is aware of the PR 'machine'?

2   Is PR a covert activity that should be made overt within media?

3   How far should PR people go in courting journalists?

CELEBRITY

In the future everyone will be world famous for fifteen minutes

—Andy Warhol, 1968

THIS CHAPTER:

↳ defines celebrity and types of celebrity endorsement

↳ considers how celebrity works

↳ describes the celebrity lifecycle

↳ considers how to measure the effectiveness of celebrity endorsement

↳ speculates on the end of celebrity.

Defining celebrity

A 'celebrity' could be defined as 'someone who is known in the public domain'. This recognition may be related to their profession or expertise: sportsmen and women (such as David Beckham and the Williams sisters), musicians (Madonna and Kylie are known simply by their first names), actors (Jennifer Aniston, Brad Pitt and Angelina Jolie) or models (Kate Moss and Naomi Campbell). These people have become celebrities due to their prowess in their chosen field.

However, there are also a number of celebrities who are known for their name, for a famous partner or simply by being exposed to the gaze of publicity. These celebrity stars (e.g. Paris Hilton, Nicole Ritchie, Liz Hurley and Callum Best) can wax and wane depending on their activities and publicists.

Some celebrities (e.g. Jade Goody) are generated by reality TV shows. Sometimes they have enduring celebrity status; more often than not, however, there can be alarming consequences for this type of celebrity.

It can be said that:

- Some celebrities are famous for what they do.
- Some celebrities are famous for not very much at all.
- Some celebrities are famous for 15 minutes.

An interesting point to note is that many celebrities are still famous long after they are dead, for example, Marilyn Monroe, Audrey Hepburn, James Dean, Elvis and (more recently) Michael Jackson. Dead celebrities can't bring any adverse publicity to a brand by their behaviour.

Celebrity management

Celebrities are brands in their own right. As such, they should have a management team who will protect their name and their brand value and generally ensure that their publicity is positive. The role of management is to nurture, expose and protect the celebrity, which may seem idealistic in today's environment. Fees and contracts are negotiated by the agent or management and can vary greatly across brands and campaigns.

Celebrity endorsement

Paid endorsement involves a brand signing a celebrity to represent the label in a traditional fashion advertising campaign. There will be a contract, which may preclude the celebrity from something as simple as cutting their hair or as complex as 'bringing the brand into disrepute'. A contract will also preclude the celebrity from endorsing a direct competitor. Kate Moss (see case study on page 81) has a large number of brand endorsements and campaigns but none of them are direct competitors. The costs of this type of arrangement are obviously greater than for other types of endorsement, such as making favourable comments about a brand in the press for a one-off fee.

Unpaid endorsement occurs when a celebrity wears the brand because they like it. The celebrity is normally given merchandise to wear at an event. This is called 'gifting'. Whilst it may appear to be unpaid, there are costs associated with this type of endorsement. One cost can be that the brand may be brought into disrepute if the celebrity behaves badly. If it is an ad hoc approach, with no contract in place, the brand has little or no protection.

The public tend to prefer covert endorsement (where it seems that the celebrity has chosen to wear a brand) to overt endorsement (where the celebrity is paid). However, the public may not be aware that behind every brand and celebrity there is a complex machine of PR working to gain exposure for a brand in whatever way is appropriate to the celebrity or the brand budget.

Companies have developed fan sites for brands, most notably on Facebook. Members of the public then become brand champions at no cost to the organisation. Word-of-mouth recommendation is a very strong and credible tool (see Chapter 3). However, these sites should be viewed with caution; they do not always make it clear if the bloggers work for the company or their PR agency and suspicion often surrounds these sites. Nevertheless, it is a growing phenomenon and gives customers a sense of affiliation and belonging to a brand. The sites often show celebrities sporting a brand.

The cult of celebrity is everywhere. Few brands do not have either an overt (paid) or covert (possibly unpaid) brand champion. Millions of magazines are sold on the basis of cover-page gossip stories regarding the celebrity of the moment. It would seem that the public have an insatiable desire to know the very latest on the celebrity circuit.

Average consumers do not readily admit to wanting to be like the celebrities they admire but they will admit to aspiring to a part of their wardrobe. They may take a leap of faith to wearing something which is inspired by a celebrity – they think that a little bit of that taste and maybe fame will rub off on them.

Brands and celebrity personalities

Brands are said to have certain personality and descriptive characteristics such as:

- classic
- fun
- bubbly
- sophisticated.

Many celebrities are also described by the public in these terms even though we do not really know them!

It is no accident that the model often described as the girl next door, who comes from Croydon and was discovered in an airline queue, is now the face of Rimmel (the first and cheapest make-up brand for young girls) and was a collaborator with Topshop (the most successful and accessible fashion-forward, high-street retailer and the first destination for millions of young girls with pocket money to spend on fashion).

Research tends to show that the use of celebrities has the most positive effect in the key youth (18–24) demographic; this reduces with age, probably because the celebrities are unknown to older audiences and they are less influenced by them.

Accidental celebrity endorsement

Sometimes a celebrity buys a particular brand and is pictured carrying an 'it' bag or wearing the brand. The brand has no control over this. When it happens, the brand is sometimes pleased to be associated with the celebrity but unfortunately there may be certain celebrities with whom the brand does not want to be associated with. The brand PR machine takes a great deal of time and effort to ensure that the celebrities they approve of are pictured as soon as possible to counteract any negative publicity. An example of this was Daniella Westbrook (a soap actor) who was snapped out with her baby, with both wearing top-to-toe Burberry check, including the pram. This picture was repeated every time there was a press story regarding the ubiquitous Burberry check, which became synonymous with British 'chav' culture. It has taken Burberry many years to shake off this association, which has a tendency to resurface every now and again to this day.

Car crash couture is a feature of *Grazia*, where a celebrity is shown wearing a style or brand which is not as flattering as would be expected. However, the brand is either unnamed or does not pay for advertising space in the magazine, as this would jeopardise their relationship. Paul Weller has worn Ben Sherman out of choice for many years and has become an unofficial 'brand ambassador'.

Some brands are very careful about the magazines to which they will send clothes for product placement or a fashion shoot. Some of the 'gossip' magazines are not deemed up-market enough to show their clothes.

Publicists and stylists spend a lot of time and energy ensuring that the celebrity and the brand are pictured together in a favourable light. Pictures of a celebrity popping down to the supermarket wearing XYZ is not just taken by chance but carefully staged in most cases; when it is not, the problems begin.

The paparazzi are well rewarded by the press for pictures of celebrities in a bad light and if they are associated closely with a brand then the brand reputation can be tarnished too. This can be a disadvantage of very close 'co-branding'.

With the advent of the Internet, particularly social networking sites and 'fans' with mobile phones, a picture can become global in very little time and the speed of dissemination can be astonishing, unlike in the past when a newspaper had time to warn publicists and agents and they in turn could 'sell' them another story to protect their celebrity client.

Theoretical background

There is not a large body of seminal research regarding how celebrity endorsement actually enhances sales of fashion merchandise. The research that does exist (identified in the list of references at the end of this chapter) tends to concentrate on other products. We can safely say, however, that endorsement is one of the most important communication channels or tools in fashion. Most academic commentators concur that using celebrities alongside products affects consumer behaviour because of transference, attractiveness and congruence.

Transference

When a celebrity endorses a brand associated with their profession (such as a sportsperson endorsing Adidas or Nike), then the theory of transference suggests that consumers will feel that some of the skills of the celebrity might 'rub off' on them if they purchase and use that brand.

Attractiveness

It is difficult to think of a celebrity who is not attractive. Nowhere is this more important than in fashion, where aspiring to look like a celebrity in terms of a hairstyle, clothing and so on allows the consumer to enter the world of the celebrity lifestyle. Young women everywhere adopt the style of the celebrities they admire. Through magazines, they are exposed to the celebrity 'look' and are given tips on how to 'get her look'. The main criticism of this has been that some young women aspire to 'be famous' when they grow up rather than having a career and they can also be influenced by celebrity diets.

Congruence

A key concept in celebrity endorsement is ensuring that there is a 'fit' (congruence) between the brand and the celebrity. It must be credible to the consumer that the celebrity would wear the brand. It does not take much for the consumer to think that the celebrity is just being paid to wear the item. Even though consumers are well aware that most endorsements are paid for, it would appear that they suspend their judgement on that unless there is a lack of congruence between the brand and the celebrity.

There have been some famous cases of celebrities endorsing a particular brand but seeming to prefer another 'off camera'. For example, a famous actress endorsed, for a rumoured one million dollars, one brand of jeans and was then photographed in a competitor's brand; she was promptly dropped from the campaign. Not only does this cost money but it costs in terms of a damaged reputation for the brand – this photograph is syndicated around the world. Whilst a contract between the celebrity and the brand can mitigate against this type of eventuality, the demand for celebrity stories is so insatiable that the paparazzi are always looking for an opportunity to expose celebrities.

Matching a brand with a celebrity is by no means an exact science. Some companies undertake research on whether the present celebrity endorsement is 'working' and into who else could have the characteristics associated with the brand (such as urban, edgy or clean living).

Sports personalities are ideal celebrities according to Stephen Urquhart of Omega as they mirror 'watchmakers who are perfectionists' (Pavri, 2010).

Our ambassadors are the epitome of mental strength and energetic passion just like Tag Heuer. We choose them for their uncompromising determination to work hard to fuel their natural talent and push further and higher the limits of their art and expertise.

This mirrors very much our watchmakers creating new breakthrough timepieces and innovating each year.

Working with ambassadors is a long term collaboration that requires deep and mutual understanding and contracts tend to be for at least three years.

—Jean-Christophe Babin, CEO, Tag Heuer.

If a celebrity stops portraying the image that fits the brand, the celebrity can be dropped and a replacement brought in. Pringle had a long collaboration with Nick Faldo the golfer. However, when Pringle re-positioned as a younger, heritage-inspired modern brand, David Beckham was seen wearing Pringle on a book-signing tour.

The Sunday Times celebrity power 50 list sorts its candidates using a combination of how many times the celebrity is mentioned in the media, magazine cover features, and Google entries and an extra dimension of what made them so popular.

The Forbes Celebrity 100 list provides a list of top celebrities by earnings.

Celebrity collaborations

A relatively new phenomenon is the 'celebrity collaboration', in which a celebrity from one world, such as modelling or music, 'develops' a range for a retailer. The most publicised collaboration so far has been that between Kate Moss and Topshop, at an initial sign-on fee of £3 million. As a globally recognised model collaborating with Topshop, which had ambitions and aspirations to develop the brand in a global market, Kate Moss became a promotional vehicle. Kate Moss and Topshop are now synonymous. To date, this has been extremely profitable for both parties.

Collaborations between designers and high-street retailers have also become ubiquitous as a Jimmy Choo range at H&M was announced and denounced equally. The collaboration between Karl Lagerfeld and H&M was not a great success for a number of reasons and one may wonder why the head of Chanel would need to make this type of collaboration.

Celebrity ranges

Some celebrities bypass collaboration with a retailer and develop their own ranges. Victoria Beckham, Caprice and Elle Macpherson have all put their names to their own ranges as they are perceived to have sufficient expertise.

Celebrity saturation

Some celebrities appear to endorse a large number of brands and the public can become suspicious, even critical, of this as it appears that they will endorse anything for money. They become known as 'brand whores'.

A celebrity can also become bigger than the brand. This has been called the 'vampire effect' – the celebrity is well recognised but the brand and its associations may be lost.

Celebrity slip-ups

When celebrities 'slip up' or fall from grace and popularity in some way by their behaviour, the brand with which they are associated is often also mentioned in press coverage. It is worse still if the celebrity is photographed behaving badly while wearing the brand. The public are obsessive in their following of celebrities, reading about both their good and bad times.

When Naomi Campbell served a community service sentence for assault, her wardrobe was scrutinised on a daily basis by the press. Even in this circumstance, a publicity machine was whirring in the background and no brand was damaged by this association. Perhaps this would prove the old saying that any publicity is good publicity. However, there are some transgressions that the public will not forgive and no amount of rehabilitation, good works and reality TV shows can resurrect the celebrity's tarnished image.

Celebrity and charities

This is a win–win situation. The celebrity is seen to be giving something back to society. The charity knows that it will get publicity if a celebrity name is associated with its endeavours.

Baume and Mercier watches are endorsed by Andy Garcia in return for his fee being donated to charities of his choice. This is a good example of celebrity and brand association for altruistic purposes. It also garners PR coverage.

CASE STUDY: Kate Moss – A phenomenon

Kate Moss (Katherine Ann Moss), perhaps better known as just 'Kate' on every magazine and newspaper headline, was born 16 January 1974 in Croydon, a suburb of London. She was 'discovered' by the founder of Storm Models, Sarah Doukas, in an airline queue at JFK airport, New York, in 1988.

Her first major campaign was for Calvin Klein in 1993. Like many of her subsequent campaigns, collaborations and coverage, this catapulted her into not just the style press but the moral spotlight as the face of 'heroin chic'. In 2007, the Forbes Rich List reported that she earned $9 million in that one year alone; by 2008, her wealth was estimated at £45 million by *The Sunday Times*. The earnings have not come from her modelling for catwalk shows alone. At 5' 7", she is relatively short for a model and her appearances on the catwalk are less frequent now, mostly just for friends. She has been the face of a great number of brands in advertising campaigns, many of them simultaneously.

Kate supports a number of charities, has dabbled in music, film and TV roles, and frequently tops the 'best-dressed' lists. The meteoric rise of Kate Moss is down to shrewd management of her image, even in a crisis. Kate is headline

(Continued)

news for any reason the press can think of, as she generates readership and sales. Even an innocent, but late, night out garners inordinate interest.

Why are the press besotted with Kate? Because the public is and she is perceived as a 'girl next door' who has turned from a gawky ugly duckling into a glamorous woman.

Kate is also a clothes horse, who is perceived to have her own style rather than being over-styled, which was obviously the attraction of her recent collaboration with Topshop. Kate Moss is cool, but to what extent is it a collaboration?

In 2005, pictures of her allegedly taking cocaine were published around the world. As publicists (such as Max Clifford) have commented, the 'outing' of celebrities is a complex business. Most publicists can keep the celebrity out of the press; they can kill the story by offering something or someone else to the high altar of public scrutiny and moral outrage. In the case of Kate Moss, who was still the darling of the press and the brands, this did not happen. Why was the story allowed to get out?

A number of reasons have been suggested:

- ↳ Because she was considered public property, the press (on the public's moral behalf) wanted to disrupt her relationship with Pete Doherty whom many considered a dangerous mismatch – it was in her best long-term interests.
- ↳ Kate had endorsed too many diverse brands and was in danger of looking like she was only in it for the money (sometimes called a brand whore). But she could not escape from the contracts without being sued for breach of contract. So she made the brands drop her.
- ↳ The pictures were a carefully orchestrated piece of publicity.
- ↳ Her popularity was waning, or would as she hit her thirties.
- ↳ The pictures were genuine and she was happy for them to be published to generate interest and reignite her career.

Whatever the case, Kate was investigated but never prosecuted – pictures cannot be accepted in a UK court as evidence when they have been sold to

(Continued)

a newspaper, so she was safe. Kate issued an apology without ever confirming the drug taking.

H&M dropped her from a forthcoming collaboration. Chanel dropped her and promptly re-instated her after the apology. Some brands did not renew their contracts; however, more lucrative contracts were signed (for example, at Longchamp).

A period of rehabilitation, not only in an American clinic but also in the press, followed. Indeed, her press coverage if anything was even bigger than before.

In 2007, Kate Moss and Sir Philip Green announced a collaboration for Topshop that was initially worth £3 million. It is understood and accepted by the public that Kate Moss doesn't design the range but authorises the collections based on her distinctive style. Indeed, it can be suggested that Kate Moss has facilitated Topshop's ambitious internationalisation process. In 2010, Kate and Topshop parted company.

Kate never speaks about anything and this stands her in good stead. It gives the press the opportunity to discuss what she might be thinking or feeling.

The celebrity lifecycle

A product has a lifecycle:

- **introduction** – designer
- **growth** – available in up-market stores
- **mass-market adoption** – available in high street stores, height of demand
- **decline** – the style goes out of fashion
- **re-arise** – return with subtle changes.

We can look at celebrity almost as a commodity, in a similar way:

- **introduction** – one to watch
- **growth and some exposure** – early recognition
- **mass exposure** – global recognition and height of demand
- **decline or withdrawal** – goes out of fashion or circulation
- **resurrection or reinvention** – return to the public arena

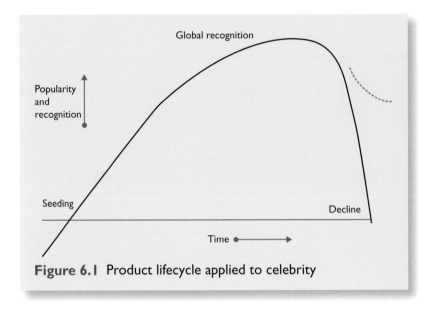

Figure 6.1 Product lifecycle applied to celebrity

One of the major and most obvious differences in looking at celebrity as a product is the price. Before celebrities reach their highest demand and global exposure, they are relatively cheap at the 'seeding' stage of their lifecycle; fashion isn't cheap at the couture and designer introductory stage of the lifecycle. Conversely, at the height of its demand in the mass market, fashion is cheap but celebrities are at their most expensive and lucrative for the brand (see Figure 6.1).

As you read the following descriptions of the stages of the celebrity lifecycle, consider the Kate Moss case study.

One to watch

Young celebrities at the start of their careers are relatively unknown and thus cheaper than more well-known people. They are people to watch for the future (also known as 'seeding') and can give an exclusive element to a brand. The only downside of this is that if they do not reach global recognition then all the investment in them will be wasted.

Eva Herzigova is a good example of this strategy. When Wonderbra had a small budget, she (an unknown catwalk model) was chosen for a billboard campaign which garnered thousands of pounds of free publicity in media coverage because of its attention-grabbing content and 'hello boys' strap line.

Seedlings grow with the brand.

Early recognition

Celebrities, at their growth stage, are becoming more exposed and well-known. As they grow in popularity and stature, brand recognition grows with them. As 'new faces', they are featured in a variety of media as no-one has yet tired of them. Lily Allen was picked up by New Look at a very early stage in her career.

Emma Watson (of Harry Potter film fame) was picked up by Burberry. Whenever she is photographed at a première or celebrity event, she is described as 'the face of Burberry', so Burberry gets a free name check every time she steps onto a red carpet. As her career will no doubt grow, so will her exposure and that of Burberry alongside. However, she may retire from public life, go to university and become anonymous. Lily Cole has gone to university and keeps up with some endorsements and modelling work. She is considered to be even more intriguing as being both bright and talented.

Global recognition

When a celebrity has global recognition, an associated brand will also become global. If it is not already a global business, it can develop new and emerging markets. Madonna and Louis Vuitton have become synonymous. Global recognition comes at a price: Nicole Kidman was reputed to have been paid £5 million for her Chanel No. 5 advert. At that cost, it is not surprising that it has been used for three Christmas promotions to date.

However, scandal is also reported on a global scale. Kate Moss suffered at the hands of the press, because of alleged drug taking, at the height of her global recognition when she was endorsing a number of high-profile brands. Some brands, most notably H&M, cancelled their contracts with her; although you may comment that this allowed her to pursue a more lucrative offer from Topshop.

Using a single celebrity who has global recognition in a campaign reaps economies of scale in terms of photography, styling and reproduction of images. A publication such as *Vogue* that has many editions in different countries across the globe can feature the same adverts and negotiate a media fee.

Decline

The popularity of a celebrity may decline because of fading public interest, changes in taste or the celebrity choosing to withdraw from the public gaze and raise a family or sheep. Celebrities grow older and very few can carry the mantle for young brands as they age. They may downsize to lesser known brands but they are forever tarred with the phrase 'the former face of' and this may be something that the previous brand would want to distance itself from so they will be paid off.

These celebrities in decline are sometimes called C-list celebrities – the last ones on the list of potential invitees to an event. Some celebrities in decline have taken up some brand endorsements which look almost desperate and lack congruence (for example, George Best and milk).

Resurrection and re-invention

There are few examples of resurrection and re-invention of celebrities in an industry such as fashion, where youth and looks are of such importance. One of the most famous examples is that of Twiggy for Marks and Spencer (M&S).

Celebrities who retire gracefully at the height of their fame seem more likely to be able to re-enter the public arena later. Those who have desperately attempted to hold onto their celebrity status do not fare so well. Reality TV shows tend to be fertile ground for celebrities to attempt to come back into the public eye and resurrect their careers but this tends to be very short term, not least because they have been out of the public eye and lost their status.

Measuring the effectiveness of celebrity endorsement

Again this is not an exact science but Mintel (Fashion and the Media, latest version) reports that a celebrity on the cover can triple the circulation figures of a magazine.

The simple advertising value equivalent (AVE) calculation demonstrated in Chapter 5 can be applied to a celebrity and a brand being photographed together. Depending upon the status of the celebrity, we can perhaps triple the AVE if the circulation of the magazine has tripled due to the celebrity feature.

Hermes, for example, does not advertise its Birkin bag. It does not need to as Victoria Beckham is always pictured carrying one and her pictures (as a wife, a mother or an invitee to an event) guarantee column inches.

The major benefits of celebrity endorsements

The major benefits of celebrity endorsement are as follows:

- **Press coverage:** Signing a new celebrity is immediately newsworthy. Journalists are always looking for column inches and know that a celebrity name gets attention. A picture of the celebrity and, of course, a picture of the new campaign is equal to free publicity.
- **Changing perceptions of the brand:** When a brand is repositioning (such as Pringle in the example above), the use of a celebrity who embodies the new characteristics is a human representation of the new values.
- **Attracting new customers:** A brand may want to attract a new group of customers, older, younger or in a new market. Asian, US and Far Eastern market entrants may use celebrities who are more familiar in those markets. Nike tends to use celebrities and sports stars that are already familiar and popular in the domestic market.
- **Freshening up an existing campaign:** Sports brands, Burberry and L'Oreal, among others, re-vitalise their campaigns by adding new 'members' to a stable of established celebrities.

The death of celebrity culture?

Commentators have been saying for some time that the cult of celebrity is over. In times of global economic crisis, it is obvious that their excesses are not being reported but their ability to sell magazines and create debate in the media and online goes on unabated. Celebrities are being shown in a more positive light in some cases when linked with charitable causes. However, in times of economic crisis, they are also providing some respite from continual doom and gloom.

Indeed, never before have there been so many different types of celebrity and the public's interest in them continues. Reports of the demise of celebrity culture have been grossly exaggerated.

Summary

This chapter has explained how celebrities are used by companies to communicate and connect with the public. The concept of the celebrity lifecycle has been developed to describe celebrities at various stages of their careers. We also discussed how to measure the value of a celebrity.

References

Clifford, M. and Levine, A. (2006) *Read all about it!*, Virgin Books, London.

Edward-Jones, I. (2006) *Fashion Babylon*, Bantam Press.

Erdogan, B. Z. (2010) 'Celebrity Endorsement: A Literature Review', *Journal of Marketing Management*, 15(4).

Lim, G. (2005) *Idol to Icon: The creation of celebrity brands*, Cyan Books and Marshall Cavendish.

McCracken, G. (1989) 'Who is the Celebrity Endorser? Cultural Foundations of the Endorsement Process', *Journal of Consumer Research*, 16(3):310–321.

Milligan, A. (2004) *Brand it like Beckham*, Cyan Books.

Pavri, S. (2010) 'Star Quality' in *Red Hot*, December 2010.

Pringle, H. (2004) *Celebrity Sells*, John Wiley & Sons, Chichester.

Activities

1   Identify a number of brands and celebrities (use visual images) and ask a small group to describe the personality of the brand and celebrities and suggest some 'fits'. If some are already collaborating, then they would appear to be a fit.
2   Calculate the advertising value equivalent (AVE) of a celebrity story or picture in the press.
3   Use the case study of Kate Moss as a basis to build on. Look at her past, present and perhaps future activities and endorsements.

THE RETAIL FASHION STORE ENVIRONMENT

We used to build civilisations. Now we build shopping malls.

—Bill Bryson

THIS CHAPTER:

↳ demonstrates the importance of the retail environment in consumer behaviour and communicating the total brand image

↳ defines the elements of the retail environment which provide these prompts to purchase

↳ describes the role of design and visual merchandising in supporting the brand image

↳ examines the role of the Internet and online shopping in relation to real stores

↳ examines the role of sales personnel in communication and transactions.

Introduction

Because it is estimated that some 70% of buying decisions are made whilst within the fashion store, it is obvious that the elements of the retail environment, at the actual point of purchase, must be important. Although we must add a caveat here that we would not know whether a store visit has been prompted by other forms of media and communication, advertising, PR, a friend or just a browsing habit. Consumer behaviour is notoriously difficult to trace in terms of influences, motivation and lifestyle.

It is in the retail environment that all of the variables of the marketing mix (product, price, place, promotion) come together in order to provide the customer with an immediate prompt to purchase. This can be called a 'trigger mechanism'. Thus, the retail environment can be regarded as the most important marketing communications tool a fashion brand has, particularly because consumers experience this environment with all their senses creating a very powerful impetus.

Visual merchandising as part of communications within the retail fashion environment can be defined as what the potential consumer sees and experiences when approaching, entering and interacting in the store. Marketing communications in the retail environment can also be considered as infotainment: part information (on trends) and part entertainment (in delighting the senses).

Consumer behaviour reviewed

To summarise the decision process a shopper goes through, it is necessary to take note of how communications in a number of forms will influence each stage of shopping behaviour.

- **Identification of need or want:** Needs and wants are established in a consumer's mind when the weather changes, a new season approaches or a new situation arises such as requiring an outfit for a special event.
- **Search:** The search behaviour can encompass a number of sources: magazines, research on the Internet, blogs, talking about trends with friends, looking at other consumers and, of course, walking around shops.
- **Evaluation of alternatives:** This can be done online or in the retail environment itself. This is a much more complex process than it might appear. It may

involve something called 'fashion maths' where the customer works out the utility value of an item based on what it will go with in their wardrobe, how many times it will be worn and how much of an investment it is – or they may blow caution to the wind and buy it anyway and worry later. They might ask advice from a shopping companion or store personnel.

- ↳ **Purchase:** At the point of purchase it may seem that there is no going back but generous exchange and refund policies, including the offer of credit facilities, can easily mitigate against any negative feelings.
- ↳ **Post-purchase behaviour:** To avoid 'post-purchase dissonance' in which the customer may feel that they have made a mistake or a rash purchase, a number of mechanisms will kick in.
- ↳ **Confirmation of the trend:** This will include searching online, in other stores or in magazines to check that the item was fashionable. Confirming with fashionable friends may mean asking friends whether it was a good purchase.

All of these stages of the fashion purchasing process are influenced by communications in or external to the store.

External communications and influences would be ambient advertising in the vicinity of the store such as billboards, street furniture, bus stops and places on public transport. The Oxford Circus underground (tube) station in London is a good example of this – the customer sees advertising for the shops they will see above ground, particularly Topshop and Nike.

External communications are often integrated into the in-store experience and would be visual replications of advertising. These act as a reminder to customers of communications they have seen before and are familiar with.

Types of store

The size and location of a store will have an influence on the types of communication which can be portrayed within a certain amount of space. However, all brands with a strong image manage to convey it, sometimes in the smallest spaces. For example, Louis Vuitton concessions in department stores reflect and are replicas of a larger store, despite occupying a relatively small space.

- ↳ **Flagship stores** are ones in which the whole brand experience and product range is showcased on a large scale. They are usually found in capital cities.

They can become destination stores in their own right and part of a tourist's visit to a city.

↳ **Stand-alone units** are smaller versions of the brand's retail environment. They may be in other major cities or in secondary locations in capital cities.

↳ **Concessions** (shops in a shop) are often found in a department store, where the brand has taken space. A concession may be operated by the brand or the department store may buy and stock a small range from the brand that suits the store's target market.

↳ **Independent stores** are owned by individuals who may be stockists for the brand.

Topshop is a good example of a retail brand that utilises all of these distribution strategies in various global locations. In London and New York, Topshop has flagship stores. In the UK, Topshop has a presence of stores of different sizes in all the major cities and towns. In the US, Topshop is rolling out stand-alone stores across several states and has also utilised a department store (Barney's) and an independent boutique (Opening Ceremony) to showcase the brand. In Australia, Topshop has tested the market in an independent boutique called Incu in Sydney before a stand alone store launch.

Store location

In general terms, the retail fashion environment is extremely competitive and the way that consumers shop in terms of fashion by browsing the available stores means that stores tend to gather and group together within age and price brands. This is known as 'adjacency'. There is evidence of adjacency on many high streets and more discrete shopping areas (for example, compare Oxford Street with Bond Street in London) but it is probably most obvious in a shopping mall environment, which, by its very nature, is a highly planned but smaller and controlled retail environment.

A new shopping mall offers a retail brand an opportunity to try out new store designs, which can then be rolled out nationwide. In many malls, it can be observed that more democratic stores such as Gap, Zara and Topshop are placed close to each other. At some distance will be the more exclusive brands, such as Prada, Louis Vuitton, Gucci, Burberry and Dior.

Westfield London is a dedicated fashion mall. Things are done slightly differently, which seems to reflect the changing nature of the fashion consumer. There are four anchor stores: NEXT, M&S, Debenhams and House of Fraser. Anchor stores are the large stores located at the 'corners' of the mall which are normally major retailers who pull in the crowds. Anchor stores tend to be located at major points of entry; in this case, they are nearest to public transport links and have escalator and lift access from the car parks. The retailers who are adjacent to these stores also benefit therefore from their location. For example, H&M and Gap flank M&S.

In Westfield London, the luxury area is called 'The Village'. The flooring, lighting and stores all have been treated to a luxury feel, it is a much quieter and more rarefied environment suited to people making purchases at greater prices. Shoppers move more slowly, there is lower footfall than in the high fashion stores but a higher spend per item. However, what sets this mall apart is that Zara and Topshop lead into the Village, which suggests that the luxury shopper will mix and match high-street, trend-led pieces with premium luxury products. The Village offers services which suit this up-market shopper, including a concierge service which can arrange the following services: language translation for overseas visitors, personal stylists, alterations, hands-free shopping and, at the end of the shopping trip, a chauffeur or home delivery.

In a traditional high street, which has evolved over many years into a high-volume, mass-market location, with various building and space restrictions, there are what we might call 'cues' to the types of store in the location for value or high-fashion brands: there will be many more, younger people, shopping in groups (pack behaviour); there will be a McDonalds; there will be little street furniture, except for litter bins; and it will be close to public transport.

In a luxury retail brand area, in contrast, there will be fewer consumers, perhaps with an older age profile; they will be shopping alone or in pairs; the restaurants will not be fast food outlets; the street furniture may include ornate benches and rubbish bins, even street sculpture. A car park will be close by, as will other services such as hairdressers, manicure bars and taxis.

There are, as ever, exceptions to these 'location' rules. These exceptions are stores that, for one reason or another, have shunned opportunities to locate in cities amongst competing offers. Value retailers such as Matalan choose cheap 'out-of-town' locations where they are a destination store and have inevitably a lot more space in which to showcase their fashion and homeware offerings. Because they are a destination store, which customers have chosen to visit, Matalan did not until recently use much in the way of display to attract customers, figuring that if they were already there, then the customers were a captive audience. However, more recently, Matalan has been improving the layouts and displays within the store environment.

Independent boutiques are often in a location which is not in the place with the highest rents. Their offer and visual treatment will be a major pull for the consumer looking for something a little bit different to the traditional high street.

Approach and avoidance

Retailers work on what has become known as the 'ten-yard rule': customers decide from a distance of ten yards whether this is their type of store, based largely on the window, the entrance and the people entering. We tend to be attracted to stores which match our personality and style, much as we are attracted to people who are similar to us.

Large windows with plenty of merchandise and mannequins are a visual cue to the consumer that this is a mass-market store; in contrast, small windows with a single mannequin with only one unpriced outfit signify an expensive store. Think of windows in a store such as Tiffany's or Bergdorf Goodman. To support these first impressions, the entrance to a mass-market store will be wide and open to cope with the crowds entering. Security guards are obvious at every entrance.

A premium-priced retailer will tend to have a small entrance; often the door is heavy and closed (it may have buzzer entry) and may be opened by a suited gentleman who is a security officer posing as a butler.

However, as usual in fashion, rules are there to be broken. Zara was probably the first store to take cues from the designer environment and translate them into a mass-market environment. They used expensive mannequins more suited to the top end of the market and these were used sparingly in the window. The entrances are slightly smaller than at Topshop, with large heavy doors, which, although normally open, are of a design more suited to the up-market stores. In store, they took this designer theme further, so much so that when they first opened in the UK, commentators remarked as much on the environment as on the prices for catwalk-inspired fashion.

Visual merchandising – the shop window

The store window is indeed the showcase for the brand. It is the silent salesperson, the visual communication tool which has only one opportunity to ensure the target market is attracted to enter the store

Unfortunately, visual merchandising went through a period of decline in which stores dispensed with the services of dedicated staff (see Lea-Greenwood, 1998) and relied upon retail staff in store to interpret centralised plans from head office. This gave rise to criticism that every store looked the same: safe and foolproof.

However, department stores and new entrants to the market (increased competition) made the market reconsider the role of visual merchandising as differentiating the offer.

Visual merchandising (along with other aspects of promotion and communication) is extremely difficult to quantify in terms of its contribution to the bottom line (turnover and profit) and therefore these artistic endeavours tend to be cut out of budgets when there is a general downturn in the market.

Today, stores such as Selfridges in London, Bloomingdales in New York and Bon Marché in Paris attract and inspire visual merchandising teams, from all over the world and at every level of the market, to study their themes and translate and interpret them for their own stores. So whilst visual merchandising remains centrally planned, it could be argued that creativity is returning.

Mannequins

Mannequins are a physical representation of the brand and can communicate in their style, pose and how they are dressed what type of store it is and what merchandise is inside (see Figure 7.1). This gives the observer an immediate cue as to whether this is the store for them.

Figure 7.1 Holt Renfrew mannequins

Themes for windows

Traditionally windows are themed for seasons, holiday periods, Valentine's day, Easter, Eid, end- or mid-season sale and Christmas – the major retail calendar event when some 30% of retail sales are made. The Christmas windows of many department stores are a major pull in their own right, providing retail theatre.

Props in display

Display props are visual symbols which support the theme and help communicate the message with immediacy. For example, a nautical holiday theme may use anchors, lifebelts, deckchairs, pebbles and sand.

Colours in display

Colours communicate and stimulate the senses:

- red for a sale
- red and green for Christmas
- black and silver or gold for sophistication.

Shape in display

Mannequins tend to fall into odd number groupings: one, three or five. Off-centre triangles can be observed in displays. They are said to capture attention as the human eye looks for balance and when it does not find it, it keeps trying, The use of odd numbers and off-centre triangle shapes means that the observer will spend more time than usual on the display. This gives a longer time for the visual communication to be effective.

From visual merchandising to visual marketing

If a store window has communicated a brand image in terms of styling and price points, then it is important that the brand promise is continued within the store, otherwise the customer can be disappointed and perhaps a little disorientated.

It is therefore a normal tactic or strategy to reflect and repeat window themes and props (accessories) in the store. This acts as a reminder to the customer of the idea which enticed them into the store in the first place.

If a store does not have a dedicated visual merchandising person or team, then plans and step-by-step guides from head office can be useful. Window themes, even in the most simple visuals, can integrate the window message with the internal and external communication. It is not unusual to see visuals which have been used in an advertising campaign repeated in windows and in store. This is part of the integrated approach to fashion marketing communications, in which the customer is reminded of and recalls seeing the brand outside the retail environment. Repetition in the use of visuals from an external campaign also provides economies of scale; a single shoot with one photographer, one stylist, one makeup artist, one group of models and one post-production process makes it very cost-effective whilst reinforcing the brand image at every possible opportunity. Images can be adapted for window displays, used internally to guide customers around the store (navigation) and on in-store magazines, look books and leaflets. They are also used in online media.

It becomes visual marketing when all aspects of the visual brand 'handwriting' are reinforced throughout the environment. Sometimes called 'bathing in the brand', visual marketing has a brand layering effect so that at any moment in time the consumer knows exactly where they are and what are the main themes and stories the retailer is communicating.

Hero pieces

One of the major ways in which stores attract consumers and convert them from being browsers into buyers is by use of the 'hero' garment.

A hero piece is a garment or accessory which is a key seasonal or directional item. It is featured in the media. In store windows and inside the store, it forms the central feature of a display. Hero pieces have a strong visual appeal.

Some hero pieces are selected by store buyers to stand out amongst the more wearable colours or versions. They are an extreme version of a trend, for example, a yellow raincoat. These pieces are attractive to and draw the customer in. These pieces do not (and are not expected to) sell in volume. This is not to say that some more innovative, trend-led customers will not purchase them.

Other hero pieces will become best sellers for the brand and will be backed up by availability and more subdued colours. In the example of the raincoat, the best-selling colours will be black, red and taupe. These are the wearable versions of the hero piece.

It is not unusual to see hero pieces in markdown at the end of the season, much like a loss leader. In fact, they have been the catalyst to sell thousands of more useful or flattering versions.

Store layout and design

There are three main types of store layout plan which are used by fashion stores: boutique, grid and racetrack. They can be used singly or in combination.

Boutique layout

This layout, shown in Figure 7.2, does not necessarily direct the customer flow in an orderly manner. Customers tend to move to the right (sometimes called the 'invariant right') when entering a store; this affects the rest of the layout of the store. Best sellers are often located to the right of the entrance but not immediately to the right, as the customer requires time to slow from walking pace to browsing pace. This adjustment of speed in the step tends to be within three paces of entering.

Boutique layouts encourage freedom of movement around the store, with fixtures blocking an attempt to walk round quickly and exit. Tables with folded merchandise are an extremely useful blocking mechanism especially as they encourage engagement with the product in the act of unfolding and touching. A boutique layout encourages the building of wardrobe displays, in which several items in a range will be merchandised together (often reflecting the window or a nearby in-store display). This encourages the consumer to build outfits and buy linked items. The first and best example of this is NEXT.

Grid layout

As in a supermarket layout, shown in Figure 7.3, a grid encourages consumers to browse the store in an orderly manner. This layout is associated with value retailers where there is a high density of merchandise. There is little space for in-store visual merchandising – the store prefers to use space for selling rather than displaying. Shopping trolleys or large baskets are provided, much like in a supermarket, to encourage volume purchasing. Primark is a good example of this.

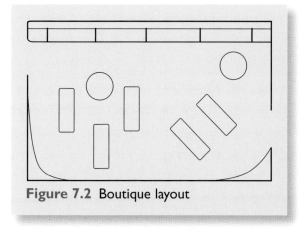

Figure 7.2 Boutique layout

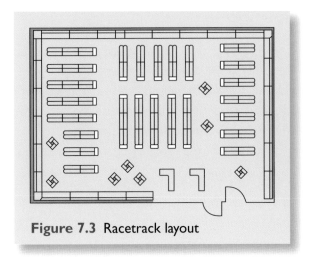

Figure 7.3 Racetrack layout

Racetrack layout

This layout style, shown in Figure 7.4, encourages consumers to move at some speed around a peripheral area which will tend to have wooden flooring. When the customer chooses which area to explore, it will be carpeted (called 'the mat' in department stores). This slows the speed down. Fashion brands in department stores are a good example of this style.

Combining layouts

Designer stores have a boutique feel but are less cluttered. They combine a partial racetrack element but this is a way of keeping customers away from soiling the merchandise – they do not encourage excessive handling. Sales personnel are there to select and place garments in the fitting room on behalf of the customer. Designer stores will have features such as fresh flowers and comfortable seating areas for tired partners.

One independent store has a 'boyfriend' area where partners can rest on leather sofas, browse men's magazines, help themselves to a cold beer from the fridge and watch the latest sports on a large plasma screen. This encourages a longer time in store as the partner is happy and amused; the longer the time the consumer spends in store, the more they tend to spend.

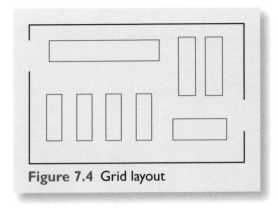

Figure 7.4 Grid layout

Fast fashion has had an enormous impact on store layouts and signage and it is not unusual to see signs such as 'get it before it goes' and 'last chance to buy' and 'when it's gone, it's gone'. These types of phrase urge the customer to action for fear that if they do not buy it now there may not be another opportunity.

A gondola fixture sometimes features one item from each range available, which suggests exclusivity, when in fact there is more stock available further into the store (see Figure 7.5).

Store design companies

There are many companies specialising in retail store design. What they all have in common is that they produce a physical representation of what is essentially an abstract concept – the brand. The environment must attract the target market, keep them in store as long as possible and deliver the brand promise.

The design company's remit usually covers the entrance, windows, wall and floor treatments, fixtures and fittings, and changing rooms. They may also be responsible for re-positioning the store. When Chelsea Girl re-positioned as River Island, few customers knew it was the same family company, the transformation from cheap high street brand to mid-priced, middle-market brand was so thorough. The repositioning was undertaken by Fitch.

Figure 7.5 A fitted-out store

Stimulation of the senses

The senses we possess help us make sense of and react to the environment around us. The sight and smell of fire, for example, alerts us to danger and our natural response is to escape. It is therefore not surprising that retailers have harnessed the power of these senses to communicate with customers.

Sight

Visual stimulation is very important in terms of colour and garment design. This is backed up by psychologists who suggest we retain 70% of what we see compared with 30% of what we hear. It could be suggested that this is the reason why advertising almost entirely comprises visual images. The in-store environment is no different – writing on signage, except for navigation purposes, is kept to a minimum. Visual stimulation is the way the environment communicates.

Touch

By handling a garment, we are, perhaps, connecting with it, which partially means imagining what it might be like to own it.

Garments which have a high touch (or engagement) factor can be strategically placed to encourage touch. Fur is obvious, although not universally acceptable. Cashmere garments are often touched and regularly held up to the neck when customers are browsing.

Blocking devices, such as tables piled with product at hand level, are invitations to touch, unfold and engage with the product.

Hearing

Music has a powerful effect on emotions and can trigger moods and memories. The music playing in retail outlets will reflect the target market's tastes, rather than being a random selection of CDs. Indeed, music has become an important part of keeping or moving customers on rapidly.

Mood Media is a company that produces 'ambient music'. According to The Sunday Times (27 December 2009):

The music that either 'seduces shoppers or drives them mad' started out as a company producing music for lifts. It grew to provide 'sensorial marketing' by producing instore digital screenings, instore radio along with instore music to suit various customers ranging from supermarkets to fashion stores. It has also now developed signature scents.

Smell

The scent of freshly baked bread has been routinely used by supermarkets to attract customers to make a purchase even when it is artificially produced (Fryer, 2011). The scent permeates the store when there is no baking actually taking place. The scents of bread baking and freshly brewed coffee are said to suggest homely qualities that are attractive to prospective house purchasers. So, it is not really surprising that fashion retailers are trying to harness scent as a stimulant to purchase.

Much like music, scent can provide an instant memory. For example, newly mown grass is associated with summer and translates nicely into crisp linens and cottons.

Abercrombie and Fitch are known to spray their clothes with their signature male or female scents so that the heady citrus mix not only attaches to you in store, but you also take part of the brand away with you whether you have made a purchase or not. Hollister, its sibling brand, does the same.

Notably, a shopping companion once remarked that M&S in Prague smells like M&S in Manchester. Whether this is intentional is debatable as M&S don't appear to use scents.

Smell is one of the key senses; it is stimulated by fragrance in cosmetic departments in every department store in the world. Singapore Airlines use 'sensory branding'. The perfume used on the hot towels and worn by the staff is called Stefan Floridian Waters. A children's wear retailer uses baby wipes with their distinctive sweet aroma to clean fixtures in the baby wear area.

Store personnel

Store personnel can be considered as the personification of the brand. Personification is when a person represents a brand concept or if a brand is described with human characteristics. It is highly likely that if you were asked to describe the people who work in particular stores, you would be describing the brand as a person.

It is quite understandable that stores aim to recruit staff who match the age, shape, style and interests of the target market. Nowhere is this more apparent than in fashion, although the same criteria can be applied to other outlets such as computer and sports stores. Store personnel can communicate the brand image through their appearance and personality, before they even interact with the customer.

Abercrombie and Fitch admit to holding 'castings' for model-type personnel to staff their stores, as do Hollister. To a certain extent, all personnel decisions on front-line staff will take into account the potential of the interviewee to represent the brand.

The case study demonstrates that stores are acutely aware of the value of sales personnel who represent the brand as a form of personification and communication and they ensure that this (unwritten) policy continues, despite any legal frameworks which might thwart their efforts. Legislation may exist to discourage retailers from recruiting by age, size, race or gender but it is unlikely that someone who does not 'match' the brand would apply for a sales position, so it becomes self perpetuating. The only times that this type of discrimination comes into the public domain are when a store repositions or decides to dispense with the services of a member of staff.

CASE STUDY

A store which underwent a repositioning exercise to move away from being a middle-of-the-road to a more directional brand alienated the staff it did not want to retain by only providing uniforms up to size 14 (rather than up to the previous size 18). Despite attracting negative reaction from the press and trade unions, the store decided that the cost of redundancy, tribunals and bad press was worth it.

Interaction between personnel and prospective consumers

In fashion stores aimed at younger consumers, the personnel do not provide a particularly personal service as the young fashion consumer is normally quite capable of browsing, locating and selecting merchandise. A personal service may be more important for older consumers or those unsure of their garment choices. Store assistants therefore need to be aware of how they are part of store communication strategies.

We have all experienced uninterested or over-attentive staff (the opposite ends of the scale). Sales personnel must recognise the type of consumer they are dealing with but, sadly, training in consumer psychology is not something that many stores have the time or budget to provide.

It is well known that sales personnel are some of the most underpaid people in retail store environments (after the cleaners) and therefore their role, contribution and potential influence on sales is also often undervalued. Commission-based retail service can be just as bad as with poorly paid staff – lack of interest may be replaced by flattery, which quickly turns to lack of interest when a better prospect is spotted.

Sales personnel can put off prospective customers and induce avoidance behaviour. However, they are often the first and only human communication tool within the retail fashion environment and really deserve a much more rigorous training programme and empowerment.

Changing room personnel

The changing room and rota duty is often the job most hated by store personnel; it is seen merely as checking people and garments in and out as a 'security exercise' but it can be the most influential area of the business. The customer has selected the garment, taken the trouble to find the changing room located at the back of the store and may be disappointed (after expending energy) that it doesn't fit or look nice. All too often, there is a lack of advice or the option of selecting other garments. The witness to this is the bulging rail of clothes waiting to go back on the shop floor. This is an ideal opportunity to interact with customers which is all too often lost.

The virtual store environment

Because the retail environment of the store itself has such a large influence on consumer behaviour, it is not surprising that the 'holy grail' of fashion brands is to re-create the bricks-and-mortar environment in their online presence. For stores which have never had a physical store environment, for example ASOS, this is not so much of an issue – customers do not have an in-store experience with which to make positive or negative comparisons. For customers who find the experience of shopping at Primark an ordeal, online shopping is ideal. Although it is a different medium, inevitably consumers will make comparisons.

There is evidence in the recent economic downturn that customers are favouring online stores so that they are not tempted into lots of stores, which increases their spending. However, many online retailers now use a tagline of 'customers who bought this, also bought that', which demonstrates that we spend more in an in-store experience, where link selling and accessorising add to the sales.

The payment experience

The opportunity to build a relationship with the store via e-mail and loyalty schemes is an important communication. Retailers can press their advantage at the point of sale by offering these opportunities.

Where there are queues, simple gestures such as apologising for the delay can be an important communication that suggests that the customer's business is valuable.

Auditing the retail environment – the mystery shopper

For many organisations, the actual reality of the retail experience is hard to quantify and judge objectively. Any visit from head office personnel tends to be announced and will encourage the store to be at its best. An increasing number of retailers are turning to 'mystery shoppers' as an objective observation of the retail environment at any given time.

The role of the mystery shopper is to take an 'experiential snapshot' of the store. This is not as simple as it would appear. It is quite difficult to take a mental note and not draw attention to oneself while posing as a 'normal' customer. Mystery shoppers are recruited from all age groups and levels of society to match the target market of different types of store. The mystery shopper will make a purchase and engage in a brief interaction. Photos taken on phones are encouraged as long as this is done discreetly.

The checklist below is typical of the areas mystery shoppers are asked to comment upon:

- ✍ **time of day/day of week:** different days of the week and times of day will give different results

↳ **general observations in the external environment and immediate vicinity:** litter, a change of traffic direction, obstructions by roadworks, maintenance, a closed store nearby

↳ **window display and housekeeping standards:** clean, graffiti free, theme adherence

↳ **in-store standards:** tidiness, staff presentation, behaviour and attitude, changing rooms, policy and cleanliness

↳ **assistance:** the shopper will ask for help

↳ **the purchase experience.**

Sometimes the 'critical incident' technique is employed. The shopper will ask about fabric composition or employment prospects, will make a complaint or request a refund, or will ask about a garment that does not seem to be available but which has featured in a magazine or advert.

Immediately afterwards, the mystery shopper goes somewhere quiet nearby, such as a café, and writes a report. He or she writes any other comments that are not covered in the checklist, which may provide the company with insights that could help make changes in training, recruitment or other areas.

Snapshots across the country can provide national and local insights which are useful for the retailer. Employees who give excellent service can be commended and win a prize, which encourages all employees to ensure that they give their best service to every customer in case they are a mystery shopper.

Future directions

Mobile phone applications are commonplace to track customers when in the external retail environment and offer suggestions regarding new ranges.

New technology allows hand gestures to change window displays and explore inventory so the customer does not even need to enter the store. This is another bonus for the time-pressed consumer.

A number of interactive mirrors are in various stages of development. Some simply suggest add-on purchases; others share choices with social media friends, so the customer can get real-time advice from friends who are far away.

Stock pads enable a customer to check size and colour availability. These are most useful in shoe shops where only one shoe is on display. Shoe stores have a much higher intensity of sales staff because they have to bring the correct size and the matching shoe out of stock.

Summary

In this chapter, the elements of the retail environment which contribute to the marketing communication of the brand have been defined.

The retail environment has been explored and explained as it is extremely important in communicating the brand image, proposition and values, at the point of sale. However, it is sometimes a neglected and underutilised communication tool. The retail environment could be said to be of paramount importance and an important tool of differentiation in what is a competitive retail fashion market. It could provide much more of a tool for communication in a crowded market of similar brands attempting to attract similar customers.

References

Fryer, J. (2011) 'Shopped! The insidious tricks stores use to part you from your money', *Daily Mail*, 1 February 2011, available at www.dailymail.co.uk/femail/article-1352392/Shopped-The-insidious-tricks-stores-use-money.html#ixzz1tmyH4KFB [Accessed 1 May 2012]

Lea-Greenwood, G. (1998) 'Visual merchandising: a neglected area in UK fashion marketing?', *International Journal of Retail & Distribution Management*, 26(8):324–329.

Activities

1   Compare and contrast the entrances, windows and layouts of a number of stores of different sizes, in different locations and at different levels of the market.
2   Access (via the Internet if necessary) the visual merchandising treatments of directional or designer retailers. Explore how they might be translated cost effectively into the mass market.

3 Observe customers in a variety of retail outlets as they are influenced by their senses: sight (visual cues), touch, smell (scents) and hearing (music).

4 Observe staff in a variety of stores at different levels of the market and make observations in terms of their personification of the brand.

5 Exchange examples of excellent and poor sales personnel using critical incident techniques.

6 Carry out a mystery-shopping exercise without drawing attention to yourself. If challenged, explain that you are carrying out an exercise for your studies.

8

TRADE MARKETING
COMMUNICATIONS

Selling to the trade is more difficult than selling to the consumer.
—Lord Alan Sugar, *The Apprentice*, BBC1, October 2010

THIS CHAPTER:

- explains how a fashion business communicates with other businesses

- describes the difference in the message, treatment and audience needs

- gives examples of fashion trade marketing communications and channels of communication.

Introduction

Communicating a brand, manufacturer or supplier to the trade is a completely different proposition from promoting to the general public and consumers. Trade marketing is concerned with a business talking to other businesses (B2B). The language, culture and process is quite different. It has different media and channels.

Julian Heptonstall of St Tropez, a commentator in the industry, said that communicating amongst the trade was 'more professional, we are talking the same language, as if we are all in this business together'.

B2B communications tend to use technical terms as the audience is more knowledgeable. It is an audience which is looking for commercial solutions. Trade journals use terms (such as 'directional', 'contemporary', 'premium', 'established', 'reputable', 'forward order', 'short order', 'sell through', 'in-season replenishment' and 'complimentary brands') that businesses use to communicate with each other. Trade journals also give wholesale prices with recommended retail prices and visual support.

There are a number of ways in which a brand, supplier or manufacturer can target the retail trade, but these will depend upon the objectives which have been decided at a strategic level (see Chapter 2).

The channels of communication include:

- trade journals
- fashion shows
- fashion weeks
- showrooms
- exhibitions, trade shows and trade fairs
- lookbooks
- events
- websites
- e-mail and social media
- in-store, point-of-sale support
- press events and releases for the trade press (as opposed to the consumer press).

Each of these channels have reach, opportunities to see, and costs associated with them.

Social media has gone some way to reduce costs and the distance between many companies and audiences. However, communicating with the trade in any way appropriate is still a key activity of many businesses.

The 'trade' can be identified as:

- **journalists** who write for trade journals
- **bloggers**
- **buyers** for retail chains, department stores and independent stores on a national or global scale
- **manufacturers, suppliers and specialists** required by the industry (such as wrapping services, promotional material, pressing equipment, and forecasting companies like WGSN)
- **the competition** at all levels of the market
- **students and academic observers** (a small but important minority, as many students cannot get access to these shows, but may be future deciders).

Retail buyers look to stock brands which will attract their target market and have a competitive edge. Manufacturers, suppliers and the various specialist service providers look to meet with buyers, brands and potential stockists.

The competition will be watching the other companies who fall within their business model: other general brands, those who are also in a specialist area (such as lingerie or sportswear) or a brand which also attracts their target market.

Press releases

A trade journalist will be looking to write about the company in order to inform retailers or an informed public audience about a brand, report recent events or ranges, and disseminate information which has been provided to them via an interview or press release. A PR agency or department (or internal press office) is expected to communicate with trade journalists and retail buyers on a regular basis. There are different ways to write and disseminate this information (see the Pringle case study).

CASE STUDY: Pringle of Scotland Cashmere

The Pringle trade press release was aimed at members of the trade who were carrying the Pringle range and at journalists. It was issued when Pringle were re-launching the brand as a fashion icon. The trade press release provided journalists and retailers with important information to give them confidence in discussing the range with their customers:

- ✎ history of the brand
- ✎ the heritage of the brand and UK manufacture and a royal connection
- ✎ product styles, fit, composition and care instructions
- ✎ personalisation options.

It can be seen that this press release and invitation to an event for journalists provides them with ready-made 'copy' to use in their publications aimed at the consumer.

The language and tone of the trade press release is quite different from that in the press release for consumer magazines, despite being for the same season's collection. The history and heritage of the brand turns into a design archive. The retail press release contains words to excite the reader with lots of alliteration, for example 'slinky thigh skimming knits', 'cult of the kilt', 'city sassiness'. Any of these short and snappy phrases can be picked up and inserted by a journalist into copy ready for the consumer to read and understand. In the retail press release, Stuart Stockdale is referred to as just 'Stockdale' – those in the know will know his full name. Like Lagerfeld, Galliano, Bailey and Dior, this raises his profile to that of a couture fashion-house designer.

Trade Press Release

Pringle of Scotland was established in 1815 by Robert Pringle whose founding principles of quality, craft and innovation continue today. The rampant lion signifies our proud heritage: Wear your Pringle with pride. Our 100% cashmere is still hand crafted at our Scottish mill in Hawick, on the Scottish

(Continued)

Borders. To keep your Pringle cashmere soft and luxurious, gently hand wash in cool water with a mild detergent. Rinse thoroughly, squeeze out excess water, pull gently into shape and dry flat on a clean towel.

The name Pringle of Scotland is synonymous with cashmere and the brand has a proud heritage of producing the finest cashmere garments. At our Hawick Mill in the heart of the Scottish Borders, we have been knitting fine quality cashmere for over 100 years.

Pringle of Scotland was one of the first brands to introduce knitwear as outerwear in the early 1900s and the first to use their signature Argyle pattern on items other than socks. Pringle is also, care of Otto Weisz its designer during the 1930s, credited with the invention of the twinset for both men and women. In 1933, Weisz also introduced cashmere as a fashion staple, one of his confirmed fans being Edward Prince of Wales.

Pringle's cashmere classics range is available throughout the year in a variety of colours and styles. Key styles include cardigans, V-neck, round neck, turtle neck, polo neck and sleeveless jumpers.

In the classics range there are two fits for women. There is the classic fit which is easy, comfortable, effortless and elegant and also the tailored fit with a slim, body skimming profile, which is tailored sleek and contemporary. For men there is also a classic fit, which is traditional, comfortable, smart and effortless plus the tailored fit which is lean and modern with clean sport detailing.

For cashmere lovers to care for their purchases Pringle have produced cashmere combs, which are perfect for removing pilling, and cashmere pearls that have been designed by Pringle and are the perfect washing product for your knitwear. To keep your Pringle cashmere soft and luxurious, gently hand wash in cool water with this mild detergent. Rinse thoroughly, squeeze out excess water, pull gently into shape and dry flat on a clean towel. In order to store your cashmere knitwear Pringle have produced satin protective covers, which helps protect against wear and tear and are complimentary from Pringle stores with each cashmere purchase.

(Continued)

At Pringle's London retail stores there is a bespoke service offering the very best of our knitwear collection custom made to your colour and style specifications and dispatched within 24 hours. In addition to this service customers can choose to have their purchases embroidered free of charge with wording of their choice.

Retail Press Release

Gentlemen prefer blondes, brunettes and red heads (in cashmere)

Pringle of Scotland present their Autumn Winter Salon Show at The Cashmere Club, held in a traditional Gentleman's Club at No.1 Whitehall Place.

This sets the scene for a collection that breaks with Scottish traditions, making new rules for kilts and knits. Mixing tailored sophistication with city sassiness, Stockdale continues to play with the masculine and feminine – hard with soft, urban and rural, new taking over old. Leather, cashmere, gold metallic and fluid ribbons.

Dusty colours and prints are inspired by Pringles 1940s archive and contrasted with dashing kilt blacks. Soft creams are punctuated with Stockdale's striking blue hues which are fresh and flirty, presenting Blue-stockinged harlots, clad in cashmere floral printed stockings and capes. A perfect mix of sexy, cosy, cashmere with a kick!

Kilts are cut up and re-located, for a tough urban world, as mini kilt capes, micro kilt skirts and scarves, sharply cut biker jackets, all in traditional black kilt cloth with leather detailing. This is the cult of the Kilt . . . as if the Kiltmaker's daughter has taken over the family business. Things will never be the same again.

For the morning after the night before, 'his favourite jumper' is re-invented as a slinky thigh skimming knitted dress. The signature Pringle Argyle is stripped away to its bare essentials – hand-knitted diamond mesh wraps around the arms, legs and body. Also capes finished with over-long fringes encase shoulders in chunky Geerong lambswool.

(Continued)

Finally traditional twinsets are stripped of their grosgrain ribbon to make fluid ribbon dresses in shimmering gold.

Autumn Winter 2003 sees Stockdale re-visit and re-invent, with playful sophistication, Pringle's glamorous heritage.

Trade journals

Drapers: The fashion business is the UK's leading weekly fashion trade journal aimed at all levels of the fashion industry trade with an increasingly global profile. It is not a journal that a consumer would purchase on a weekly basis or subscription. An online version, www.drapersonline.com, provides a daily digest of the most up-to-date news from the fashion industry. *Drapers* covers clothing, footwear, lingerie and accessories alongside articles on issues that are of most concern to the fashion industry at any given time, including manufacturing, advertising, careers and education. It provides classified advertising for jobs, services and brands. The journalists at *Drapers* and Eric Musgrave, their most influential editor for many years, are renowned for taking on board and discussing the issues which are uppermost in the fashion retail industry.

Drapers hosts a 'fashion summit', an annual conference each autumn that attracts high-profile speakers and delegates. Other conferences for the industry are about specific subjects, such as 'e-tailing' or e-commerce. *Drapers* also gives out its own fashion awards every year at a very prestigious event honouring brands and retailers from all segments of the market and major figures in the industry in its lifetime achievement awards.

A content analysis of *Drapers* demonstrates that an issue normally contains:

- editorial on an issue of the moment
- news roundup
- comment and analysis
- features
- classified advertising
- recruitment opportunities.

Other specialist journals exist, for example *Jewellery Buyer*, *Bridal Buyer*.

Fashion shows

Individual companies may put on a fashion show which is aimed at their store management, their partner stores and their stockists. These events are normally covered by trade journals but not by mainstream magazine media.

At a fashion show, a company has an opportunity to showcase their new season range, give ideas for visual merchandising and may offer seminars on selling techniques and product knowledge.

Franchise operators, such as Benetton, often use this as a communication tool. Franchise operators in overseas markets, such as NEXT, invite partners to see their collections at their head office. This gives the franchise partners an opportunity to see how to showcase the collection.

Press shows can include a fashion show where the press preview the forthcoming new season. Marks and Spencer (M&S) show the press their Autumn–Winter collection in July in order to prepare the press for the arrival of the collection in store in August.

Fashion weeks

The London, New York, Paris and Milan fashion weeks are a major feature of the fashion communications calendar. They have been joined by emerging markets, such as Shanghai and Istanbul, in recent years.

Fashion weeks have become a brand in their own right and attract sponsorship, which also gives publicity to the sponsors. The main sponsor of London fashion week is the British Fashion Council and other sponsors include companies that are not necessarily fashion related but provide a supporting role to the industry as facilitators, for example Vodaphone, Canon, American Express and DHL.

These are high-profile events as they showcase the trends which will filter down to the high street. The audience will include trade buyers from department and independent stores, newspaper and magazine journalists, stylists, influential bloggers, buyers, other designers and, of course, the celebrities on the front row (FROW) (Figure 8.1).

Figure 8.1 Celebrities on the front row (FROW) at a fashion show

Fashion weeks are reported quite differently in the trade journals and the mainstream consumer media. Trade journals give coverage to colour palettes, silhouettes and the more technical aspects of tailoring or fabric composition; mainstream journalists point consumers to new trends. Trade journals profile the designer or brand and give information on lead times, minimum order pieces and wholesale prices.

Showrooms

Showrooms are a major communication tool for fashion companies. They are often laid out beautifully to showcase the brand at its best. There is professional photography on the walls, comfortable seating, and a high standard of refreshment options. A showroom may look just like the flagship store environment (see Figure 8.2).

In a showroom, buyers can look at the whole range, decide what suits their target market and make forward orders for the coming season. Showrooms are staffed by dedicated and skilled personnel who know the brand, the image, the customer

Figure 8.2 A display in a Ralph Lauren showroom

profile and the key (or hero) pieces that are going to be featured in the press. They can advise on other brands that the range can sit beside. They can also decide whether a retail store is suitable for the brand and can refuse to stock certain stores.

Showrooms often host events for journalists and trade buyers. These can be low-key, drop-in, daytime events or more lavish and expensive evening affairs. At a shoe event co-sponsored by Piper Heidsieck (the champagne brand), attendees were given a champagne glass in the shape of a shoe and a small bottle of champagne (see Figure 8.3). In this case, influential style and fashion journalists were also targeted to begin to namecheck Piper Heidsieck in their copy.

Companies that cannot afford a dedicated showroom in a capital city may have a dedicated space in a shared showroom or use the services of a PR company. Companies may substitute or supplement their showroom presence by having a 'trunk show' in a hotel or other accessible space. (In earlier days, travelling salesmen would carry samples of ranges around in a suitcase, hence the phrase 'trunk show').

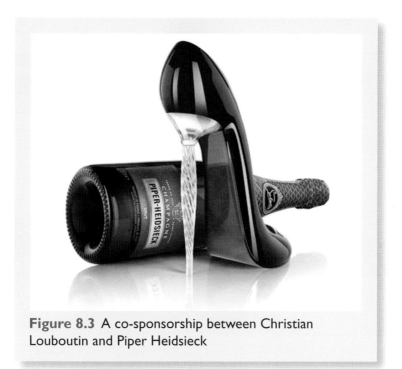

Figure 8.3 A co-sponsorship between Christian Louboutin and Piper Heidsieck

Exhibitions and trade shows

Today, in an increasingly virtual world, much information is available on the Internet. However, trade shows and exhibitions have a long history and a continuing role as a showcase for the fashion industry and as networking events:

- They can specialise in product categories.
- They bring many people and brands together in one space that can be missed in a clicks (Internet research) environment.
- The competition can be observed.
- They showcase many brands in real, live, three dimensions that allow buyers to touch and see the fit.
- They communicate personally with potential buyers.
- They provide 'educational' opportunities with seminars.
- They provide a networking and social opportunity.

The calendar of trade shows for fashion tend to be around similar times, to help the forward-order buyers. Collections for Spring–Summer 2013 will be exhibited in late summer 2012. Some exhibitions are seen by buyers as 'must go to', some are new exhibitions to watch and some are relatively small or new.

The following list contains some of the many exhibitions:

- ✎ Menswear exhibitions
  - ❍ Pitti Immagine Uomo, Florence
  - ❍ Stitch, London attracts 6000 visitors and runs parallel with Pure
- ✎ Womenswear exhibitions
  - ❍ Prêt á Porter, Paris
  - ❍ Pure, London is one of the most well-known of the UK events. As well as 1000 womenswear fashion brands at every level of the market, it also offers accessories and footwear thus providing retailers with an 'opportunity to diversify or compete with the high street'. There are seminars from fashion experts, catwalk shows, networking and drinks receptions over the three days.
- ✎ Men's and women's exhibitions
  - ❍ Moda, Birmingham includes lingerie, swimwear, footwear and accessories.
  - ❍ Gallery, Copenhagen is popular with independent retailers.
- ✎ Childrenswear exhibitions
  - ❍ Pitti Immagine Bimbo, Florence has 500 brands and averages 11,000 visitors.
- ✎ Streetwear exhibitions
  - ❍ Pure Spirit, London showcases 300 trend-led brands and runs in parallel with Pure. It includes catwalk shows, free breakfasts, networking events, and specialist seminars on topics such as visual merchandising and social media. This demonstrates that a trade show is more like a conference, networking and educational opportunity for independent stores, department stores and larger retail chains.
  - ❍ Bread and Butter, Berlin celebrates ten years (in 2011) as one of the most influential trade shows. It has changed the face of traditional stands in massive halls. The exhibition stands are like art installations in their own right (see Figure 8.4).
- ✎ Footwear
  - ❍ Micam, Milan is 'the most important fashion footwear show in the world' with some 40,000 visitors.
  - ❍ Magic, Las Vegas
- ✎ Specialist
  - ❍ Premiere Vision, Paris is the most famous and well-attended event, showcasing the latest trends in shape, colour and technical innovation to the textile trade.

Figure 8.4 Hilfiger stand at B&B Berlin July 2011

○ Pitti Immagine Filati, Florence showcases knitwear yarns.
○ The London Textile Fair.
○ Eclat de Mode, Paris specialises in fashion jewellery.
○ Fast Fashion Tour, London is a new show that is responding to the trade's need for access to fast fashion.

In the current trading environment, trade shows have had some problems recruiting exhibitors and attendees, because of financial constraints; however the main ones appear to have a loyal following. One observation is that fewer company representatives are being sent and one or two people may have to collect information and observations on behalf of the whole company. Many trade shows are reluctant to reveal visitor figures; part of this may be that not all visitors are in a position to make decisions – they may merely be collecting information. Bread and Butter say that the senior buyers (the decision makers and order writers) attend.

Recently, more specialist trade shows have been joining the trade show calendar, due to retail and consumer interest in the issues. The ethical sourcing trade show and Eco Chic New York (see Figure 8.5) are examples of these newer shows.

Figure 8.5 Specialist trade shows for: a. ethical and b. ecologically sound fashion

CASE STUDY: Where fashion meets art

Scoop is a relatively new fashion trade show based at the Saatchi Art Gallery, London. It advertises that it is 'minutes from the city's best retail spots and gives a brand exposure to the most influential buyers and press in the industry'. This is a new type of event which has a smaller and more personal feel compared with the enormous exhibition halls.

The buyers, competitors, manufacturers and media are professionals who are distinct from a consumer audience, in that they are looking at the brand from a commercial viewpoint.

Selling space at a show is also a business and a lot of design goes into the sales pack and stand application (Figure 8.6) that encourages companies to take a stand.

Figure 8.6 Sales pack and stand application

Trade marketing stands

The stand at a trade show is the communication tool for the brand. There is fierce competition to have the most engaging and exciting stand.

Stand personnel

The people who 'man' the stand are the front-line communicators of the brand or service and they should be friendly, articulate and knowledgeable. The brand owners or CEOs are the best ambassador for the brand or service as they are passionate about it. The appearance of an influential figure (such as Renzo Rosso on a Diesel stand) garners a lot of publicity.

Any models hired to wear a brand (see Figure 8.7) should be more than simply an attractive addition. They should be fully briefed in order to represent the company. A member of the team who is a sample size is often a cheaper and more knowledgeable option.

You should avoid having friends dominating the stand, availing themselves of the hospitality. It is there to attract potential business contacts.

Figure 8.7 Hilfiger models

Lookbooks

A lookbook is a glossy and often expensive publication (Figure 8.8) that serves as a trade communication tool. It gives potential stockists and journalists reference numbers, colour ways, size options and wholesale prices, along with visuals ready for point-of-sale material and photo shots.

Exhibition stand builders and visible/invisible costs

Exhibition stand builders can create simple exhibition cases or more sophisticated sets, working in conjunction with design companies.

Some of the most sophisticated stands at Bread and Butter are said to cost in excess of £250,000 to build. This is the visible cost. Promotional gifts, manning

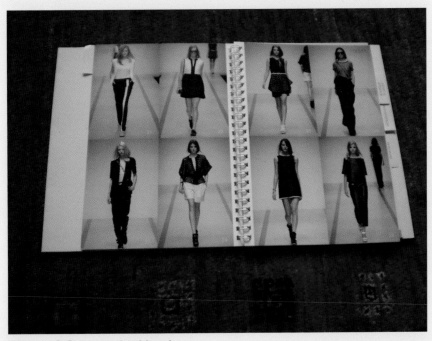

Figure 8.8 Jaeger lookbook

Figure 8.9 Goody bags in my car

the stand, hospitality, models, music systems, DJs and choreography can all be considered invisible costs that add to the overall costs (in the region of £500,000) of appearing in the exhibition.

Promotional gift merchandise

Promotional gifts are an important part of the trade or fashion show experience. In exchange for a business card for the database, most visitors appreciate a gift, which makes an emotional connection and can open a conversation.

For fashion shows and press events, gifts are often known as 'goody bags' (see Figure 8.9) and may consist of a combination of free samples and publicity material.

Pens, sticky notes, pen drives (USB memory sticks), sweets with a logo and stress balls are commonplace now and they have to be superior to those handed out by the competition. It is worth looking to source a promotional gift which becomes a 'must have' item and a talking point.

Gifts which stay on a desk (such as paperweights) or are carried around (such as key fobs, suit protectors and umbrellas) are a permanent reminder of the company or event. Baseball caps are popular at urban menswear exhibitions; however that may also mean that they are too common a sight.

For the fashion industry trade visitor, the item must be a useful gift, relevant to the company and, above all, tasteful. Figure 8.10 shows a promotional gift which

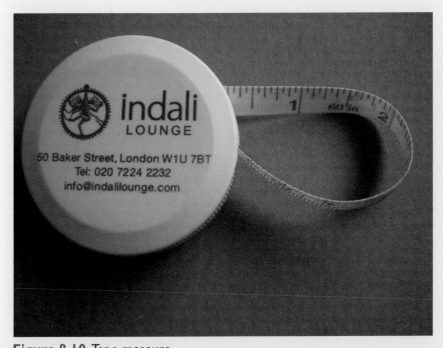

Figure 8.10 Tape measure

is given to guests at an Indian restaurant in London. It may seem strange, at first glance; it is an unusual device to keep a restaurant in the mind of a customer. However, the restaurant is opposite M&S head office on Baker Street and it is highly likely that suppliers, designers and the press are taken there for hospitality events.

Events

The trade holds a variety of events to communicate with present and potential retailers or stockists and the press.

Types of event include:

- breakfast meetings
- showroom receptions
- awards and drinks receptions at conferences, trade shows and fashion shows.

After-show parties are sought-after invites and often covered in the press

Journalists, and more recently influential bloggers, are invited to the brand show-room where the PR staff (either in-house staff or an external agency) can explain the brand philosophy and the new collection. Press packs include hard copies of the press release, pictures from the lookbook and gifts, as appropriate. The information is also transmitted electronically.

It is essential after an event of any description that guests are thanked, asked to give feedback on the information and hospitality and are entered into the company database. Many companies begin a dialogue that specifically addresses the needs of the buyer or press contact.

Websites

Company websites usually have separate sections that are clearly aimed at the consumer, at the trade or stockist and at the press. The language used in these sections will vary according to the audience.

E-mail and social media

Trade companies use a variety of ways to gain contacts to form a database. At trade shows, visitors and browsers are encouraged to leave a business card and have the opportunity of being entered into a prize draw. This gives the company a list of contacts for future B2B marketing activities via e-mail.

Social media has become an important communication tool as it is personal and immediate. Facebook is becoming an important tool for gathering 'friends' and disseminating information, which can then be shared with other 'friends'. Noor by Noor is a Bahrain-based fashion business which has used Facebook very success-fully to communicate with customers and the trade at relatively low cost.

Tweeting and blogging are also important tools of communication during an event, as influential stylists communicate and drive footfall to a stand or event. Bloggers are becoming as important as the press and celebrity guests on the front row at fashion shows.

Supporting the trade

Long after a trade event, the merchandise arrives in store. It is extremely impor-tant that the brand supports what is known as the 'point of sale' for communica-tion purposes. This can include a number of initiatives:

- posters
- wrapping materials
- display props for visual merchandising
- mini lookbooks
- postcards.

All of these initiatives support the brand in the store environment.

Summary

This chapter has explained the difference between B2B and B2C communications in the trade dimension of the fashion industry. It has also given examples of fash-ion trade marketing communications and channels of communication.

Activities

1   Access some of the websites of trade shows and companies mentioned in this chapter.

2   Access trade and consumer communications for some brands of your choice. Make a list of the key words the trade uses when communicating with other businesses (B2B) that differ from the ones it uses when communicating with customers (B2C). This is a content analysis methodology.

3   Write two types of press release: one aimed at the trade and one aimed at the consumer journalist.

4   Describe how you might organise an event for the trade, an exhibition space, a fashion show, a meeting in a showroom or a breakfast event. Fully cost the event.

INTERNATIONAL FASHION MARKETING COMMUNICATIONS

. . . besides that was far away and in another country

—Shakespeare

THIS CHAPTER:

↳ explains the factors
  that influence fashion
  companies to venture into
  overseas markets

↳ gives examples of cultural,
  consumer and climatic
  constraints as points of
  difference for marketing
  communications

↳ discusses the
  regulatory frameworks
  for international
  communications

↳ uses a case study on
  Bahrain to explore
  issues in mounting a
  communications campaign.

Introduction

Operating within the domestic market is familiar and often safe; however operating and communicating in a new and unfamiliar market brings with it a number of challenges, not least in terms of communication strategies.

The international consumer

Some similarities exist amongst certain homogenous groups and this can facilitate global campaigns, particularly for luxury brands. For example, a business man aged around 30 who lives in London, Paris, Milan, Tokyo, Shanghai or the Middle East may wear a Hugo Boss suit, Church's shoes, a Rolex watch, Armani underwear, Nike sportswear and Givenchy aftershave and carry a Paul Smith briefcase. Young women shopping in any of these cities may also be part of a homogenous group. What separates these groups are the cultures in which they live. There are differences in consumer culture that will affect their behaviour and are the key to understanding how to communicate with them.

Global Blue (www.global-blue.com), a tax-free shopping company that provides shopping guides for all the main fashion cities of the world, launched a new publication called SHOP in spring 2011 in 26 countries simultaneously. The content is one-third advertising and two-thirds editorial. It is also available online and has a phone app to calculate tax refunds. Contributors are journalists from all the major high-profile magazines. It has maps of shopping areas that show the location of every store and gives translations (for example, the London guide has Chinese, Russian and Arabic translations).

Operating outside the domestic market

Increasingly fashion brands are moving into overseas markets. This can be online or in retail stores. Push factors encourage companies to expand out of the domestic market into overseas markets; pull factors pull companies into new markets.

Push factors

Push factors are elements or conditions that make further expansion in the domestic market difficult. These factors can relate to increased competition, falling profit margins, changes in consumer tastes, government regulations or pressure from institutional shareholders to seek higher returns through expansion to new markets. At an organisational level, overseas expansion may be driven by the ambitions of a senior management team who want to follow the competition or become an international business.

Market saturation occurs where there is no further growth potential in the market and the possibility of improving profitability is limited. This may be a reflection of market conditions or a declining business format. Under these conditions, a brand has a store in every viable domestic location and can see no further opportunities in the domestic market. This lack of opportunity may result from a combination of factors over which the company has little control:

- recession
- regulatory conditions, such as planning consents
- increasing corporation tax or the minimum wage
- demographic influences, e.g. aging populations.

Pull factors

Pull factors relate to the attractiveness of overseas markets rather than the lack of attractiveness of the domestic market.

Opportunities may exist to gain higher operating margins than in the domestic market as a result of lower levels of competition, less government regulation, a gap in the market or better supply chain conditions.

Economic conditions may cause an overseas market to grow in affluence and consumer demand, as seen in Brazil, Russia, India and China (the BRIC nations). In China, the growth of an affluent middle class is driving the demand for international fashion brands.

A new market may offer relatively little in the way of regulatory barriers to entry and in some instances will positively encourage market entry through incentives.

Some developing markets have a younger demographic, which is attractive to fashion retailers. There are a number of ways of looking at which markets are attractive to companies that are internationalising. Much will depend on the companies' corporate objectives, the degree of fit between these objectives and the conditions which exist in the potential new markets and the company having the infrastructure (such as offices in key locations) to serve overseas markets. Developed western markets may be culturally similar and appear to be relatively easy to enter but may already be saturated.

CASE STUDY: Topshop

An example of how push and pull factors have impacted upon a company's internationalisation is seen in the case of the UK company Topshop entering the US market. Topshop tested its products in the market using department store concessions and a capsule collection in a boutique called Opening Ceremony.

Topshop can be seen as being pushed out of the UK market – it has stores in every location that can support the business, its demographic has peaked and fewer malls are being built.

Topshop was pulled into the US market – it was talked about by celebrities and journalists, there was little competition for the business model (fast fashion) and its British fashion forwardness was welcomed by US customers. This was exploited in marketing communications: the store is known as Topshop London and features iconic British symbols, such as the Union Jack, red London buses and red post boxes.

Chicago was Topshop's next stop after opening the flagship store in New York.

The UK market has proved an exception to the notion of a saturated market. It still attracts overseas entrants and international fashion brands. The market has been open to foreign direct investment and has proved a popular market for international fashion brands. The UK is often described as fiercely competitive yet it is attractive, as the consumer is hungry for fashion.

CASE STUDY: Forever 21

Forever 21, a US-based fast fashion retailer opened in Birmingham, UK in November 2010 and in Dublin, Eire, soon afterwards. These might be seen as 'soft' openings to ensure that any problems were ironed out before opening the London flagship store in late July 2011, which garnered the most media coverage. They state that they will have 100 UK stores within five years in 'every major city, every mall, and every major high street' (*Drapers*, 29 July 2011).

In terms of culture, the UK has what might be called a secular environment. Forever 21 uses religious Christian texts in its promotions and printed on carrier bags is the Biblical reference John 3:16. The company says this is a statement of the family's personal faith but separate from the business. This promotional logo may need to be adapted for the Islamic countries it intends to enter in the future.

Making such a declaration of faith may inevitably attract scrutiny of the way the company deals with workers and suppliers (BBC Radio 4 discussed it in *You and Yours* on 29 July 2011). A number of websites are dedicated to discussing the low-priced operation.

Emerging markets

An emerging market is a current growth market where economic development is driving rising standards of living and creating increasingly affluent consumers while significant numbers of the population still live at the poverty level. Literacy levels are low and communication infrastructures are underdeveloped outside of the industrialised cities. Developing integrated communications campaigns is more problematic because of the geographic size and spread of these markets. Some markets, such as Cuba, are almost impossible to enter because of political constraints. Other markets, such as the less politically stable African markets, have not yet seen a sufficient rise in consumers' disposable income to warrant entry by fashion retailers.

A. T. Kearney (www.atkearney.co.uk) is an international management consultancy group. It publishes an annual retail development index that shows the relative potential of retail environments based on four variables of: risk, saturation, attractiveness and time pressure. This gives retailers a good indication of the markets they should be scanning and deciding the ones to enter and the ones to avoid at the present time.

Benetton entered Cuba in the early 1990s and opened five shops. Benetton had seen this market as a long-term strategy so that, when rationing of clothing ended and disposable income rose, it would have 'first-mover advantage' and be seen as a desirable brand with which Cubans were already familiar, even if they could not afford its products previously. However, it has recently closed two of the stores, which may mean that the opening of the local market has not come to fruition as quickly as they expected.

Developing versus developed markets

Companies have to make a decision whether to enter markets which are developing but which may not have an infrastructure that mirrors the one in the domestic market. Eastern European markets may have some cultural similarities in terms of consumer taste and fashion appeal, which makes market entry easier, but all markets have unique features and cultural similarity cannot be assumed. This is important for developing communication strategies which reflect the local culture.

Companies need to develop communication strategies that transcend culture or are significantly adapted to meet the needs of specific target markets in terms of cultural norms. Middle and Far Eastern markets are not culturally similar to western markets and the retail operation will need adaptation including communications, in order to comply with local customs and culture.

One of the things that these potential markets have in common is their cultural difference and distance from the west. When it comes to entering, operating and communicating in these countries, adaptations have to be made to many aspects of the marketing mix to suit the local market:

- **Product:** differences in sizing, seasonal changes, variations in climate and colours.
- **Price:** differences in import duties or taxes.
- **Place:** retailers may operate from shopping malls and department stores.
- **Promotion:** for some markets, a standardised campaign can be used – if a global campaign is used, some subtle changes will still be made by the brand.

One of the main ways in which retailers entering overseas markets attempt to overcome these cultural differences is by partnering with a local company. This is mandatory in some countries.

Overall, fashion retailers looking to internationalise should keep in mind the 5Cs:

- **customer:** lifestyle and attitudes towards fashion (for example, Australia has a more casual and sporty approach to fashion).
- **culture:** adaptations of clothing and its communication in the media to fit in with, for example, local religious constraints.
- **competition:** retailers already in the market and the adaptations they have made.
- **climate:** a key issue for clothing, much more than for other products.
- **constraints:** the regulatory frameworks of owning, operating or communicating the fashion range.

Warmer or colder climates can often be used to test ranges which may then show signs of being best sellers and the company can react quickly and appropriately. NEXT and Marks and Spencer (M&S) are known to test their summer ranges in the Middle East. Fred Perry produced warmer jackets for the Russian market, which they then introduced to the UK, EU and US markets.

When Topshop first internationalised into Australia, they did this by 'testing the market' using a concession in a Sydney boutique called INCU; however it was soon discovered that they did not take the climate into account and were sending the wrong season's items. Topshop later set up an international division in the UK head office to more accurately target the consumer in these culturally and climatically different markets with their different constraints.

Franchise operations are a popular choice for western brands entering Middle and Far Eastern markets. The overseas partner takes all the risks and benefits of operating the brand in the new market as they can help the retailer adapt to the local consumer, culture, competition, climate and constraints.

The Alshaya group is one of the biggest franchise operators covering the Middle East, North Africa, Turkey, Russia and other countries from the previous eastern bloc nations. They have over 80 nationalities in their workforce, which they say gives them an advantage in understanding cultures and the needs and desires of particular markets (www.alshaya.com). As a franchise partner, the Alshaya group can advise and adapt the marketing mix to suit the local market.

International regulatory frameworks

All governments control communications, to a greater or lesser extent: what can and cannot be said in advertising products. These controls may be laws or regulations. In the UK, the Advertising Standards Authority states that all advertising must be legal, decent, honest and truthful. The Chinese government censors Internet content. Most countries have adopted some form of self regulation except for those countries which are heavily influenced by religious laws or where dictatorships and communist regimes remain.

These regulatory frameworks require some level of adaptation to be made to communication campaigns especially for global and pan-European fashion brands. Each market needs to be investigated individually and assumptions should not be made.

Most countries have in place a regulatory framework that outlaws fraudulent or misleading advertising, sometimes called the 'hard' issues (Copley, 2004). The major cultural differences which affect fashion retailers entering culturally diverse markets are sometimes called 'soft' issues; however they are often just as important.

Religion

The use of religious symbols and creative treatments are sensitive in many markets. For example, Benetton's use of two nuns kissing caused outrage in Catholic countries. Islamic law has very strict regulations on the use of the female form in any type of communication including advertising and window displays.

Representation of women and children

The role of and objectification of women is an issue in some countries and can cause an advertisement to be withdrawn form the market. However, in some countries, such as France, the use of the naked female form is widely tolerated.

Advertising using children or aimed at children is banned in some countries, for example, in Sweden.

Language

In France, as an attempt to maintain the integrity of the French language, advertising has to be translated. The NEXT strap line 'bringing fabric to life' was translated quite literally into 'resuscitating dead material', which was not exactly the image the company wanted to portray.

French Connection (using the fcuk logo and strap line) came under scrutiny in a number of markets. The scrutiny was probably one of the reasons that French Connection resurrected the full name of the company in many of the overseas markets it was penetrating, facilitated by selling thousands of T-shirts with the fcuk slogan in the domestic market.

Taboos and customs

As part of religious constraints, certain countries have taboos which would not be immediately apparent to some creative fashion marketing teams. They can include the use of sacred symbols (cows and crucifixes) or unclean animals (pigs) in either the product or the communication strategy.

Nike inadvertently used the Arabic symbol for Allah on a running shoe, creating a furore on two counts. Using the name on the feet is seen as demeaning, insulting and highly offensive.

In Thailand, showing the soles of the feet is considered highly offensive. This would affect a company such as UGG whose advertising is based around footwear.

Standardisation and adaptation in international fashion marketing communications

If every aspect of the marketing mix is replicated in every market in which a company operates, we describe the company as adopting a strategy of 'standardisation'. Complete standardisation would mean producing the same products and selling them at the same prices in identical outlets supported by a single communications campaign. The major benefit of standardisation is economies of scale – it is much cheaper per item to produce a large number of identical items, whether they are products for sale or marketing materials.

However, standardisation of a marketing mix in international markets is quite rare. Even luxury brands, which could be considered to have a 'global' image, make subtle differences to product colours and prices, the method of distribution and the marketing communications, to suit the target market.

When changes are made to the marketing mix to ensure that the offer matches the consumers' needs in terms of the 5Cs, we describe the company as adopting a strategy of 'adaptation'. The major benefit of adaptation is that the company ensures that its offer is more closely targeted, but it can cost more money in terms of processes.

All companies tend to use a combination of standardisation and adaptation in their marketing mix and particularly in their communications.

Standardisation: Levi's

Iconic denim brand Levi's is renowned for its creative marketing campaigns. In the late 1980s and early 1990s at the time that it was internationalising across Europe, Levi's used the global language of classic youth and US soul music tracks with visuals of the minutiae of US life to communicate its classic brand 501. The adverts were screened across Europe simultaneously and created such demand that 501s sold out. The first and most well-known of these adverts was 'Launderette' utilising the song 'Heard it through the grapevine' originally sung by Marvin Gaye. Today these classic adverts are viewed regularly on YouTube.

It is interesting to note that Levi's deemed it too risqué (self regulation) to show Nick Kamen (then an unknown model) strip down to a pair of Y-front underpants on terrestrial TV screens across Europe so they were substituted with boxer shorts which launched a revolution in men's underwear in their own right. Calvin Klein built its brand on them.

In August 2011, Levi's launched its first truly global campaign utilising the social media channel Facebook, which was followed by cinema, print and outdoor media. Global chief marketing officer Rebecca Van Dyck said that across 19 countries 'people can share it, they can talk about it' and 'it's extremely exciting to have one voice, one message and it seems like the right thing to do because our consumer is global' (*Drapers*, 29 July 2011).

Adaptation: H&M

H&M can be considered a global brand as it trades from around 2200 stores in over 40 countries. H&M has collaborated with a number of high-profile designers and celebrities over the years. Each of the collaborations (with Lagerfeld, Madonna, Comme des Garcons, Versace and, more recently, David Beckham) coincided with H&M's expansion into the home markets of the designer or celebrity. Despite a collaboration with Kylie Minogue, the Australian market has yet to be conquered although there is a Facebook petition called 'Bring H&M to Australia'.

The pages on www.hm.com are adapted for each individual market. This is most apparent for markets such as Saudi Arabia, where the clothes shown are very conservative and modest. H&M TV shows a number of short films with local designers, for example, Lulu Han who is a designer in Shanghai, taking the H&M crew around the local sights.

Brazilian model Gisele Bundchen's Spring–Summer 2011 campaign for H&M was a global standardised campaign and coincided with H&M's entry into Brazil. However, because of external pressure, this image was adapted for the Middle Eastern market by airbrushing and using Photoshop, according to *Campaign* (21 March 2011). A T-shirt was added to the image for the Middle East, to cover exposed flesh.

In Figure 9.1, a magazine cover acceptable in the French market on the left is digitally manipulated to make it acceptable for the Middle East. This makes the use of the celebrity and one picture shot economically viable.

General considerations for international marketing

Franchise partners are normally useful for local contacts and agencies. Most of the big media agencies over recent years have either acquired or incorporated local advertising agencies in order to gain an understanding of the economic and regulatory conditions and opportunities.

Figure 9.1 Adjustments are made to images for use in different markets

Channels of communication in overseas markets

TV, radio, cinema and the press are often controlled by the state in developing markets. This will impact on the choice of media channels and the creative treatments which may or may not be allowed.

Celebrity endorsement is an obvious example of adaptation to an overseas market. Nike is one of the companies that selects celebrity endorsers which are familiar to the individual market.

Product placement is differently regulated in different markets. From 2011, the UK has allowed product placement in TV programmes as long as it is extremely clear. This is not always the case in overseas or developing markets.

Objectives of international campaigns

Campaigns will tend to fall into one of the following scenarios: introducing the brand to the new market, keeping the brand in the public eye and responding to any adverse publicity.

In the domestic market, the brand is established and known to the target audience. Upon entering an overseas market, new customers will need to be alerted. Advertising, events, and public relations activities are required to engage with the media, fashion stylists and customers. When entering New York, Topshop had to take a lot of time and effort to introduce the US customer to its offering.

Depending on the nature of the entry strategy, the brand may not have a large presence in the market: there may be a small store or a concession in a department store. In contrast, the brand might have a larger number of stores, a nationwide presence and consumer understanding in the domestic market. Coverage in the fashion press is to be encouraged after the initial entry stage.

Just as in the domestic market, brands have to be careful to ensure that any negative publicity is dealt with quickly. Local partners are instrumental in facilitating this. Cision is a worldwide PR agency operating in over 150 countries, with local personnel so they can advise on any cultural factors which may impact upon communications.

However, mistakes can still be made by companies. Agent Provocateur is a brand that elicited a number of complaints in the Middle East for window displays in Dubai and, more recently, in the emirate of Sharjah, which, although near to the commercial city of Dubai, is considerably more conservative than Dubai. Agent Provocateur windows were showing lingerie on mannequins with facial features. In Sharjah, the decency laws passed in 2008 decree that mannequins should be headless and that clothing displayed should be 'decent' (*Gulf News*, 29 December 2010). Since this negative publicity, it has become clear that Agent Provocateur has tried to engender public support by encouraging positive press coverage of events across its Middle Eastern markets.

International communications in the digital age still require some careful thought; it is clear that whatever is available virally or globally on the Internet may still be subject to cultural constraints.

Summary

This chapter has explained the factors that influence fashion companies to venture into overseas markets. It discussed the varying international regulatory frameworks and gave examples of cultural, consumer and climatic constraints.

Whilst the fashion market or industry is often called 'global', it is clear that many markets are different in terms of their stage of development, demographic, incomes and consumer sensibilities. They often need an adaptation of fashion marketing communications.

References

Copley, P. (2004) *Marketing Communications Management: Concepts and Theories, Cases and Practices*, Elsevier/Butterworth Heinemann, Oxford.

Mueller, B. (1995) *International Advertising: Communicating Across Cultures*, Wadsworth Publishing Company. Belmont, CA.

Activities

Consider the Bahrain case study and carry out these activities.

1 As a new fashion brand entering Bahrain, design a campaign to announce your arrival. You will need to consider the 5Cs introduced in this chapter.
2 Which cultural barriers or regulatory frameworks might you face in Bahrain?
3 As a fashion brand that already trades in the kingdom, design a year's promotional plan for Bahrain.
4 What types of event would you look to sponsor in Bahrain?
5 How would you assess the effectiveness of your promotional efforts?
6 Which other aspects of the marketing mix need to be considered to inform your promotion?

CASE STUDY: Bahrain

The Kingdom of Bahrain is a relatively small island principality with a population of 1.2 million, ruled by the Al Khalifa royal family, which makes up the majority of the parliament. Founded on oil wealth and pearl production, Bahrain is now a major financial centre, considered to be growing faster than many other parts of the Middle East, and has become more liberal than many neighbouring emirate countries.

(Continued)

Eight million tourists visit Bahrain per year, mostly from other Arab states, but increasingly from elsewhere. This is due to Bahrain's investment in infrastructure, hospitality, art and culture, retail and world class events, such as Formula One.

Bahrain dubs itself as being 'business friendly', a modern country with 'Gulf glitz' yet having 'authentic' Arab culture. Islam is the dominant religion as some 80% of the population are Muslims. However, there are a small number of other religions practiced including Christianity and Judaism. Friday and Saturday make up the weekend. There are a number of national holidays in addition to religious festivals, such as Ramadan. Arabic is the indigenous language but English is used widely. The demographics indicate that 517,000 of the population are guest workers from India, the Philippines, and Sri Lanka. Almost 90% of Bahraini women are unemployed. Women were given the right to vote in 1999 and there has been some evidence of them gaining more roles within the workforce. One of the attractive market features of Bahrain is that it enjoys a tax-free shopping environment.

Direct inward investment is not possible in Bahrain. All overseas players entering the market have to have a local partner. A form of franchising is frequently adopted in order to facilitate distribution. The benefit of a local franchise partner is that such companies seek to achieve promotional goals on behalf of the franchisor. They are well placed to ensure that Islamic cultural regulations are upheld when interpreting international campaigns. Additionally they have on-the-ground knowledge of the best retail locations and shopping malls. The main partners, amongst others, operating on behalf of international 'fashion' companies are: Alshaya, Al Hawaj and Jawad.

Promotional opportunities for fashion, beauty and lifestyle in Bahrain include:

- state-owned TV and radio
- magazines: *Bahrain Confidential*, *Shout Confidential* (a younger version of *Bahrain Confidential*), *Grazia* Middle East edition, *Fashion Bahrain*, *Woman*, *Ohlala!*, *Areej* (Arabic)
- *Gulf Insider* (a men's magazine)
- newspapers: *Gulf News* (the major national newspaper, which includes lifestyle supplements)

(Continued)

↳ billboards: numerous ambient advertising opportunities along roads and on lamp-posts
↳ sales promotion: discounts and offers, shopping festivals, high days and holidays.

Public relations is relatively new to Bahrain and is based on magazines and events. Direct marketing is not favoured as mail delivery is not well covered but text and e-mail are an important channel. The Internet and social media are not as well used as in other countries, as access is state regulated.

As a franchise partner, Al Hawaj is sent ready-made pieces of artwork and communications by the overseas brand owners. Al Hawaj interprets the communications based on their local knowledge and some of them are adapted by a local media company owned by the family. A significant amount of the communications budget is then spent on major events, such as Three Hot Days (July), Jewellery Arabia and Eid. Other events are related to Royal Ruler's day, shopping festivals, and religious holidays.

In developing a communications campaign, an important consideration is that the company does not have as sophisticated data as is available in the UK, therefore the process of accurate targeting and market position- ing is more difficult. Significant differences exist in terms of the choice of communication channels. Print media advertising has been growing for the company but television advertising is not as significant because of costs and the fact that there are only two stations owned by the same company. Other media channels are radio stations, which reach the youth market. Al Hawaj is known for its charitable foundation, which helps create a stronger brand profile. In Bahrain, for Al Hawaj the most effective media channels are street furniture (in particular, billboards and lampposts) within the shopping malls, Other media, such as magazines, remain relatively cheap. Although online advertising has not been fully exploited, it has great potential for the development of social-networking sites, which creates an opportunity for many forms of digital advertising. However, online access is state regulated.

(Continued)

Bahraini consumers want to see and be seen. They have a very straightforward response to advertising and respond to brands. There has been major growth in advertising, particularly on billboards on major highways; billboard advertising is the preferred medium for many consumers, followed by print media. In a survey conducted by Yasser Al-Hawaj, 65% of those interviewed liked SMS advertising as long as it did not become 'too much'. They did not like flyers and mail shots, considering them 'cheap'. They also did not think that online advertising was used much in Bahrain yet. Consumers say that they like luxury product advertising. Research evidence also suggests that they are responsive to promotional material as they see it as a form of entertainment.

The data in this case study is adapted for the purposed of class discussion and activities from a dissertation submitted to Manchester Metropolitan University by Yasser Al-Hawaj (2010).

10
REGULATORY FRAMEWORKS

Some advertising will offend some of the people, some of the time.

—Anonymous

It is not surprising that an industry such as fashion attracts what might be considered more than its fair share of complaints because of its image-based promotional techniques.

THIS CHAPTER:

↳ explains the regulatory frameworks applied to fashion marketing communications

↳ outlines the major issues which are of importance to the regulation of fashion promotion

↳ explains the role of the consumer and the regulatory authorities

↳ gives examples of communications campaigns which have come under scrutiny.

Introduction

The fashion industry is no stranger to controversy over its advertising because of its propensity to shock, show nudity and play with sexuality and sexual orientation. Overall, it has a need to stand out in an increasingly saturated and competitive retail fashion environment.

It is not surprising that fashion companies sometimes push at the boundaries of what may be deemed acceptable. However, advertising is said to reflect current cultural concerns and this can open a healthy debate on the subject.

There is a self-regulatory framework administered in the UK by the Advertising Standards Authority (ASA). This is based on codes of advertising rather than on laws, although legislation may cover some aspects of misleading claims, racist or sexist imagery or language in advertising. 'Self-regulation' means that, by and large, it is left to the industry and the public to 'police' the adverts to which people are exposed. According to the ASA codes of conduct, all advertising must be: legal, decent, honest and truthful.

The ASA covers advertising in:

- **print media** (magazines and newspapers)
- **broadcast media** (TV, radio and cinema)
- **sales promotions** (including direct mail, e-mail and SMS messages)
- **the Internet** (an area which is increasingly being complained about).

There are clear legal frameworks, such as the Trade Descriptions Act, which can protect consumers where misleading claims are made about products. There are no specific legal frameworks to protect consumers from advertising that may cause individual or collective offence.

Advertising must not commit any serious or widespread offence against generally accepted moral, social or cultural standards or offend against public feeling including race, religion, sex, sexual orientation or disability (ASA). This can easily be seen to be a subjective and difficult area to regulate, not least because many fashion companies see themselves in a creative and artistic industry.

The role and remit of self-regulation

The ASA recognises that advertising informs and often also entertains. It sees its role as one which ensures that the public are not offended or misled. It is particularly mindful to protect the young, the vulnerable and the less educated in society.

To this end, just one complaint will trigger an investigation, which means that any single member of society (an individual or a member of an organisation) who finds an advert offensive has a right to make this known. The ASA receives an average of 26,000 complaints per year of which around 10% are 'upheld', which means that the ASA agrees that the advertisements are not acceptable.

The panels of the ASA, which consider any adverts that have been the subject of complaints, are made up of a combination of advertising specialists and lay people. The funding for the ASA comes from a levy on all types of advertising, which means that 0.1% of the cost of any type of advertising is directed towards the ASA to enable it to undertake its valuable role. It is not funded by the government.

At any given time, the ASA has what it calls 'hot topics'. These are issues of the moment that often lead to updates or changes to the codes of advertising. The ASA responds to societal changes and can adapt to changes in promotional techniques much faster than a legal framework via parliamentary acts ever could.

The ASA has a comprehensive website which shows examples of adverts which have been banned. The ASA's adjudications can be searched by industry sector.

Hot topics in the fashion industry

This section deals with recent hot topics related to the fashion industry. In the process of responding to complaints, new guidelines have developed over time. In many cases, they are still developing as the ASA responds to consumer complaints and the industry's continuing competitive marketing approaches.

Cosmetics, facial and body enhancements

Technological advancements in post-production, known as the 'digital enhancement' of adverts has led to an increasing number of complaints concerning airbrushing of photographs. When a cream to combat the aging process is being advertised, removing fine lines is now banned. 'Before' and 'after' pictures must not be enhanced. Highlights added to photographs of hair products which claim glossy properties are not allowed. Airbrushing models to make them thinner is an on-going debate. This comes under the remit of misleading and irresponsible images.

If lash inserts and hair extensions are used on models, the viewer must be advised of this on the advert. This is also an ongoing debate as recent complaints have concerned the font size and position of the disclaimer on adverts.

Sexualisation of children

Children are defined as those under 16 years of age, but sometimes further broken down into under-8s and those between 14 and 16, which may reflect cultural changes in children's developmental stages. It is generally accepted that children should not be exposed to physical, mental or moral harm. They are vulnerable to advertising because of their lack of intellectual development.

Sometimes known as the 'Lolita effect', the sexualisation of children is a hot topic on which the ASA has asked for some research so that it can be well-informed as it draws up developments to the codes of advertising. Meanwhile the ASA responds to complaints and bans adverts that break the present codes. A recent example is a girl's T-shirt with the slogan 'nothing tastes as good as skinny feels' (see the ASA adjudication on Zazzle Inc, August 2011).

Size zero

There are ongoing complaints about airbrushing or deliberately using underage and underweight models, which, it is claimed, gives young women (and, increasingly, young men) false ideas about normal bodies.

The fashion industry has tried to take a stand on this and has incorporated certain self-regulations regarding the age and body mass index (BMI) of models. However, there are still many instances of the self-imposed codes being flaunted, often without the designer's knowledge. Diana von Furstenberg outlawed models under 16 on the catwalk but found out via the media that one model was 14.

Lord Smith of Finsbury, the chairman of the ASA, said 'I was left with a firm impression of how media literate and savvy these young people were, and how fiercely they felt, as well, about what was acceptable and what wasn't in the ads they encountered every day. It was a reminder of how important our work is' (ASA, 2011).

Environmental claims

The ASA say the 'green area is a rather grey one'. Environmental claims in advertising have also come to be known as 'greenwashing' the public. This suggests that many companies are making claims about their green credentials, such as environmental processes in the production and distribution of clothing, which they may not be able to substantiate. Indeed, much evidence to date suggests that the public are neither well-informed nor sure about what many of these claims mean.

Violent imagery

An increasing number of complaints concern the inappropriate use of violence, either actual or implied, in advertising. This has prompted a research report and a seminar held by the ASA, which has led to a strengthening of the codes. In particular, there are issues when the use of violent imagery in fashion advertising is said to glamourise knife or gun ownership or use (ASA, 2007).

The process and progress of a complaint

The majority of TV and radio adverts which will have a wide reach are 'pre-cleared' by the ASA, particularly where the company or advertisers think that they may have crossed a line in the code. This will often be at pre-production stage based on a storyboard or script (to avoid expensive production costs). In most circumstances, this is straightforward. Sometimes the artistic production changes and this is why the public are sometimes incredulous that an advert has been allowed to be shown.

Due to the sheer volume of other advertising media, the ASA does not have the resources to pre-clear it and relies on the public to draw their attention to any advertising which appears to break the codes. Companies who have shown a continuing disregard for the codes have to have every advert or piece of promotional material vetted. This is a direct result of being banned in the past. In fashion, this applies to Diesel and to Dolce and Gabbana at the time of writing.

Once a member of the public has complained about an advert or any type of marketing communication (online, in writing or by phone), a process starts culminating in one of the following 'adjudications':

- ↳ no case to answer
- ↳ informal resolution
- ↳ not upheld
- ↳ upheld (banned).

The complainant remains anonymous throughout the process and is kept fully informed of the process.

A panel is asked for an initial judgement, which may decide that there is no case to answer as no codes have been broken. Informal resolution is also a speedy process where the advertisers are told about the complaint. They may adjust the advert accordingly, as happens for many minor breaches of the codes.

If a case is deemed to warrant investigation, the advertisers, the agency and the medium in which the advert appeared are all asked to comment upon the complaint. The media are asked comment because very often the public complain to them rather than to the ASA. This gives extra evidence of complaints which may have been filed.

The panel meets (in person or electronically) to discuss the code which has been broken and the context in which the advert has been shown.

For example, an advert for Opium perfume by YSL Beauté Ltd showed a reclining naked model. This was acceptable in fashion magazines, but not when it transferred to giant billboards viewed by all the public. This was termed widespread offence and was upheld. The case against the advert appearing in specific, fashion-focused magazines was not upheld.

Communicating the results of adjudications

The complainant is given advance notice of an adjudication. This is subject to an embargo and the published adjudications appear every Wednesday.

The press pick up on the adjudications and may discuss them. Commentators say that this gives the companies more free press coverage and, whilst it may be negative press, it is still a form of publicity. These adverts might never have come to widespread attention and the companies are courting free publicity by deliberately creating offensive advertising and using shock tactics. There is a fierce debate around giving the 'oxygen' of publicity to adverts which are banned.

However, the ASA says that there are some negative consequences: continual breaking of the code means that all future advertising has to be pre-vetted; the media in which the advert appeared also gains negative attitudes by association; advertising agencies may suffer if companies remove their accounts from them; and the public do remember the negative adjudications.

International considerations

As many companies are engaging in an international retail environment, the use of integrated campaigns and standardised approaches towards promotional material to gain economies of scale from centralised divisions may also cause international complaints which may not occur in the domestic market.

It is therefore necessary that international sensitivities are considered by companies. To facilitate this, Burberry, for example, employs a number of nationalities in their London creative team. Debenhams has recently appointed a German-speaking marketing executive to facilitate its entry into the German market; part of the job description was to interpret cultural differences. Franchise partners in markets known to be culturally sensitive, such as the Middle East, give advice to the companies they represent there.

Where the problems seem to lie

Advertising agencies are very well aware of the codes of advertising. It appears that most problems occur when the creative teams employed in-house (for the company or the media, for example, in fashion shoots) work with famous photographers and without advice from an agency. Mario Testino made his name with the Benetton advertising that caused widespread offence in the 1980s, which is still quoted today in any debate concerning shock tactics.

It is often noted that fashion companies engage an agency either to create their advertising or to advise them when they have transgressed the codes and come under the scrutiny of the ASA.

However, much of the debate concerns the extent to which advertising reflects society and should be allowed to do so to create a record of sociopolitical influences. This is similar to the debate around art movements in the past, where some pictures were banned from public display.

The UK is renowned for its creative, ironic, iconic, humorous and entertaining advertising and therefore wins many international awards. Despite the fact that there are sometimes calls in Parliament for more specific legislation to counteract inappropriate advertising, the process of self-regulation appears to be working very well at present.

Summary

This chapter has described the role and remit of self-regulation in fashion marketing communications. The process of complaints and resolution is described. The international aspects of regulatory frameworks are discussed further in Chapter 9.

References

ASA, www.asa.org.uk.

ASA (2007) *Advertising and Young People*, June 2007.

ASA (2011) *What you looking at? Drawing the line on violence in advertising*, November 2011.

Activities

1   Familiarise yourself with the ASA.
2   Complain about an advert and observe the process and final adjudication.
3   Discuss issues in the ASA's list of hot topics.
4   Discuss the oxygen of publicity given to banned adverts.
5   Does a regulatory framework stifle creativity?

11

ASSESSING THE EFFECTIVENESS OF FASHION MARKETING COMMUNICATIONS

I know that half my advertising budget is wasted but I don't know which half.

THIS CHAPTER:

- ✏ looks at how the effectiveness of the tools of a promotional campaign can be measured

- ✏ discusses outline methods adopted by industry specialists which can be used to support traditional quantitative and qualitative measurement variables.

Introduction

In the world of fashion marketing communications, where brands face a competitive retail environment, it is no surprise that companies want some evidence of how their creative campaigns have achieved their objectives in terms of increasing sales, changing consumer attitudes, establishing a new brand or reinforcing the image of an existing brand. These are all difficult areas to test in terms of effectiveness.

It would be simplistic to suggest that effectiveness can be measured by the number of people who have seen an advert. It may not be relevant to them, they may not have registered its content or they may have screened out the message. This is called selective perception. A consumer may pass billboards, posters or digital advertising boards or open a magazine or newspaper and still not register the content or message, as media messages become part of life's daily clutter. The challenge for the marketer is to ensure that the message and the brand name enter the consumer's consciousness. One way of trying to establish the extent to which this has taken place is to try to measure the effect of a campaign.

Effectiveness may take several forms including raised brand awareness, facilitating brand switching, the communication of a new fashion range or more measurable outcomes such as sales increases, which can be seen in an improvement in the bottom line. A return on investment can be measured in incremental sales over a specific period of time. However, some campaigns may only increase sales for the duration of the promotion – over a year, the same amount of the product may be sold as usual. However, what if the aim of the campaign was to re-position the brand in the mind of the consumer or to change perceptions of the brand? This would require more long-term research in terms of a tracking study to see whether the effects of the campaign were sustained or lasted only while the campaign was running.

It is widely commented that it is extremely difficult to assess how advertising works; indeed many people are reluctant to admit that advertising affects them at all and yet millions of pounds are spent on advertising and promotional campaigns every day.

YouTube has a wide selection of adverts for people to view. Some of the interest in this site is about acknowledging classic advertising campaigns, for example,

Levi's adverts – 'Launderette' is probably the most popular, combining as it does humour, music, nostalgia and a young male model. Other adverts accessed also seem to suggest that the public enjoy the entertainment of adverts. So advertising is not solely about selling but is also about entertainment. This may complicate the commercial–creative dichotomy.

Models of advertising

In order to understand effectiveness, we first need to understand the way in which advertising works. A model is a simple way of explaining a complex process (think of the reality of the London underground compared with the simplicity of the model – the map).

One of the earliest models of how advertising works is the AIDA model, a linear model of a complex process that attempts to demonstrate how a consumer moves from awareness to purchase. The model suggests that consumers pass through four stages before making a purchase:

- **Awareness or knowledge (cognition):** The consumer becomes aware of a brand or product as a result of one or more elements of a communication campaign: advertising, online communications, in-store promotions, PR or billboards.
- **Interest (affect):** The consumer responds positively and likes what they see or hear.
- **Desire:** The consumer wants to try or purchase the product.
- **Action:** The consumer moves towards an intention to buy.

One of the major problems with models of this type is attempting to understand how the consumer moves from awareness to action and what influences this behaviour. Advertising or promotional messages are normally encoded in some creative process. How consumers decode them is not as linear as we might be led to believe by textbooks. The public's reaction to an advert may include liking it but not necessarily decoding it enough to purchase the product.

People have a complex set of memories, influences and needs which impact upon purchasing behaviour. Indeed, the case study on page 167 shows a linear series of events and, to any observer, the consumption behaviour would seem to be bizarre and not to follow normal purchasing behaviour.

Measuring effectiveness against campaign objectives

Companies should have a set of achievable objectives for a campaign, agreed with the agency or in-house function (see Chapter 2). It would be unreasonable to expect a campaign to achieve more than is possible. Achievable objectives should have realistic and specific targets, such as:

- increased footfall
- increased average spend
- increased sales of a specific range e. g. coats
- raised brand image
- reinforced brand image
- introduction of a new brand or sub-brand
- repositioning of the brand.

Any one campaign will not necessarily have all of these objectives.

Campaigns that aim to change consumer perceptions may include the following objectives:

- confirming our fashion credentials
- being foremost in the consumer's mind for ski wear
- attracting a wider range of consumers.

All campaigns must be underpinned by research before and after the launch. Research can be done on either a continuous or an ad-hoc basis depending on the speed with which the campaign needs to be put together and the resources the company has available in terms of people and finance.

Research can be done through secondary sources, such as market reports published by specialist agencies (for example, Verdict and Mintel) or through trade magazines (for example, *Drapers*) that provide quick and easy access to relevant industry information and consumer attitudes. More in-depth research can be carried out through fieldwork, otherwise known as primary research. The research can be carried out through the following types of organisation:

- external research consultancies (Mintel and Verdict)
- an internal research function (the brand's own marketing department)
- the advertising agency (a department that is often called 'insight').

Pre-launch research

This type of research will include a full audit of the fashion brand. A SWOT analysis is useful. Consumer perceptions of the brand will be collated to demonstrate weak areas. From this, a campaign with measurable and achievable results will be formulated.

It is essential that a brand undertakes research prior to engaging with an advertising agency, so they have a clear idea of what they want from the process. Otherwise the brief given to the agency will be weak and the chance of achieving its objectives limited.

Ongoing research

Snapshot research of the results will be undertaken during the life of the campaign. This will give the brand an understanding of how the campaign is reaching its target and may lead to a change of strategy; magazine advertising may perhaps increase and TV advertising be scaled down. If viral marketing through a blog, a chat room or a banner campaign has been utilised, the impact of digital platforms will be seen more quickly and the focus of a campaign may switch to increase the use of digital platforms.

Post-campaign evaluation

Research undertaken after the running of a campaign will try to measure the results against the objectives which were set at the beginning of the campaign. The results of the research can then be used to formulate future strategy and determine how the momentum of the campaign can be maintained. It is important that a brand continues to be represented in the various media or the interest which has been generated will dwindle and die as new brands come to the market or competitors increase their promotional activities.

Assessing the effectiveness of traditional media

The way in which effectiveness is measured in traditional media is based on coverage (opportunities to see or hear), day-after recall and brand awareness. However, positive results may not necessarily convert to intention to buy. Indeed, effectiveness may not necessarily convert into increased spending. Many texts would suggest that recall has an effect on consumer behaviour, particularly in terms of memory, attitude and perceptions towards a brand.

First, we consider quantitative approaches used by specialist industry agencies which contribute to the measurement of effectiveness. There are a number of independent specialist agencies that collect media-specific data on viewing (TV), listening (radio), admissions (cinema) and circulation (newspapers and magazines). In the UK, these agencies are as follows:

- **Broadcasters' Audience Research Board** (BARB, www.barb.co.uk): This agency collates data on the number of people watching particular programmes. It is perhaps not surprising that the top programmes on commercial TV channels (where advertising is allowed) are reality TV shows, soap operas, sports and films.
- **Radio Joint Audience Research** (RAJAR, www.rajar.co.uk): This agency collates data on the number of people listening to commercial radio stations.
- **Film Distributors' Association** (FDA, www.fda.co.uk): This agency collates data on cinema admissions figures.
- **Audit Bureau of Circulations** (ABC): This agency collates the circulation data on daily, weekly and monthly publications.

What these agencies have in common is that they enable the advertiser to see the most effective places to advertise their brand through the identification of target audiences and their listening and viewing habits. One consequence of this is that advertising costs relate to the size of the audience or the potential reach of the campaign.

For example, *The X Factor* attracts an audience of around 12 million per week. NEXT has used the commercial break to launch its Autumn–Winter campaign. Because of the high advertising costs for a prime-time television slot, only one coat is featured for 30 seconds. If viewers go online to watch *The X Factor*, they are exposed to a three-minute advert for Next showcasing a number of styles of coat including men's and children's wear. Regional variations can be defined by the data; in the past, Next has used this to good effect by targeting its advertising in northern regions where sales increased substantially.

Viewing, listening and circulation figures therefore give us data on numbers of people, based on secondary data that has been gathered by specialist agencies on an ongoing basis through quantitative approaches. This data helps in the process of media selection, finding the most effective form of media for the chosen target group.

Targeting in the cinema

As discussed in Chapter 2, cinema audiences for a particular film tend to be a homogenous group with similar ages and interests. Advertising can, therefore, be targeted more precisely than general family viewing. For example, fashion, beauty and fragrance advertising dominate films such as *The Devil Wears Prada*. There was an obvious symbiotic relationship between the film and Chanel as Chanel was a major theme of the film.

There is a fine line between media saturation and consumer fatigue. Marks and Spencer (M&S) continually add new celebrities to their advertising campaigns to maintain the momentum.

Targeting in newspapers and magazines

Newspapers and magazines are highly targeted and the advertising will tend to reflect that. For example, luxury brands often do not allow press samples to be featured in weekly chat or celebrity gossip magazines, however celebrities snapped in luxury brands often feature (and the brand has no control over that). The advertising or promotional features that appear in a broadsheet, such as the *Financial Times*, will differ greatly to those in a tabloid newspaper.

Grazia can be considered as one of the most democratic magazines, where luxury rubs shoulders with the high street.

In general terms, newspaper circulation is falling, particularly for daily newspapers. This may be due to a number of variables, such as people having less time to read a newspaper and the availability of news instantly on the Internet. Circulation figures set advertising rates, however, it is acknowledged that magazines are read more than once and by more than one person, so readership figures become important here. Magazines are looked at an average of 2.3 times.

Qualitative research

Qualitative research is based not on numbers (such as viewing figures, opportunities to see or circulation figures) but on studies of consumer attitudes and behaviours. It seeks to establish not 'how many' but 'what' opinions and attitudes are held by consumers. It is a valuable way of establishing shifts in consumer attitudes after a communication campaign, or before a campaign in order to establish consumer perceptions of a brand and the extent to which those attitudes need to be changed in order to persuade the consumer to buy.

Qualitative research can take the form of observations, focus discussion groups or depth interviews. Qualitative research allows consumers to express in their own words their attitudes and beliefs. The value of this type of research is that it can reveal beliefs about a brand unknown to the marketer and not previously considered. For any communications campaign to be effective, these views need to be known at the outset of any campaign.

Cinema

Cinema audiences can be targeted immediately after a film to discover what aspects of the adverts they recall. This gives advertisers an indication of which parts of the advert (which will normally be cut for a TV commercial) would be the most memorable.

Magazines

Consumers looking at magazines have been observed and researched, which has demonstrated how consumers use them. This has given us data which shows that readers pay more attention to the first third of the magazine, to the right-hand pages and to adverts close to or opposite a 'newsworthy' story often called 'matter' (Chapter 4 gives more detail on the power of magazines).

From this research, we can choose where our advert will go. Of course, the advertising rates for specific sections of a magazine reflect the potential effectiveness in terms of consumers being more receptive to the advertising (or product placement).

Focus groups

Focus groups gather a small group of 5–7 like-minded and similar-aged people to test their individual and collective perceptions towards a brand, product or customer service. Normally focus groups are carried out by trained facilitators. Focus group research can give advertisers an understanding of how their brand is perceived before, during and after a promotional campaign.

Levi's uses focus groups to plot where the brand sits in consumers' minds in relation to their competition. They are also used to pilot test Levi's adverts.

CASE STUDY: Consumer perception

A company producing organic cotton wool was finding sales very slow despite being stocked by major UK supermarkets and the obvious consumer interest in natural products produced without bleaches, pesticides and so on. The company asked a research company to try to work out why.

A focus group was convened of women who had expressed that they preferred to buy organic products to use on their own and their babies' skin. Word association for cotton wool brought out an overwhelming use of words such as white, clean, fluffy and soft.

The organic cotton wool product in its opaque packaging was shown to the group and they were asked what they expected to see inside the package. They almost all responded that they suspected it might be off-white and rough to the touch. The respondents were then invited to open the package and they were most surprised that the product was indeed white, fluffy and soft. The company changed to see-through packaging and saw sales rise exponentially.

Depth interviews

These are one-to-one interviews conducted with consumers based on open-ended questions. They try to draw from the consumer their attitudes towards a brand or their beliefs about the brand. These interviews can be carried out in the consumers' own homes or in the offices of research agencies. Depth interviews can reveal the strength with which a consumer has a positive or negative perception of a brand. Additionally, they allow more probing of opinions either direct or indirect. One method of indirect probing is a word association test used in a focus group or on individuals. This is a research method which aims to establish a descriptive relationship associated with the brand. Some of these words may then become part of the brand's image encoding. For example, respondents may be asked to associate the brand with an animal, an adjective or a colour.

CASE STUDY: Impulse buy

In a fashionable French ski resort, a woman enters a boutique, selects a black fox fur-trimmed Prada jacket, checks the label, goes to the till and pays 1200 euros. She leaves her old ski jacket to be disposed of by the store, puts on the new jacket and leaves the store. The process has taken less than ten minutes.

The literature would regard this as unusual consumer behaviour. In order to understand how this rather speedy and seemingly random purchase has been influenced by any internal and external factors, the researcher would have to take something called a 'protocol statement' from the consumer. By interviewing the consumer, we may understand the internal influences (such as memory) and the external influences (such as the media) on the purchase.

The protocol statement taken from the consumer stated: The friends in the ski party had been laughing at how old the woman's jacket was during the previous few days. The day before the purchase, she had spent some time looking at various jackets and the Prada one, although expensive, was considered to be most useful. It could be worn both in the ski resort and in winter in the UK as it resembled a normal jacket. Furthermore, the woman remembered seeing a similar jacket on Victoria Beckham in a magazine and liking it. So she had 'slept on it' and decided that this jacket would be perfect for her holiday and her home and work lifestyle. The day before the purchase, her son was with her in the boutique and said, 'Oh, Mum, treat yourself'. The woman confessed that although she did not actually ski she

(Continued)

felt better walking around the resort in her new jacket. All the friends in the party had admired the new jacket.

It is clear that there were a number of influences at work which could not be observed during the purchase. To do this type of research with consumers is both time consuming and expensive but it does give a richness of data from which advertisers can attempt to understand how the consumer mind works and may be able to exploit these influences.

Other methods of determining effectiveness

Recall and recognition tests

There are a number of ways of undertaking this type of research; again this can be done in a focus group or with an individual. This may be day-after recall, which can then be repeated at larger time intervals to see whether the level of recall is the same over time and with and without prompts (aided or unaided recall). Recall may start wide with 'can you tell me which fashion adverts you have noticed recently?' It then may focus on asking for recall of specific advertising.

Recognition tests may ask respondents to identify an advert without seeing the brand name. Respondents may view the advert with the name and then be asked whether they can remember any particular details.

Eye-tracking studies

A camera can be attached to consumer's head to track the movement of the eyes when browsing a magazine. The data shows how long the eyes rest on a page. This technology was originally developed for supermarket research and produced data on the most effective positions to place products in store. It has recently been developed to use eye tracking when looking at a computer screen to assess the effectiveness of adverts, advertorials, web pages and product placement features.

Figure 11.1 shows how gazeplots and heatspots demonstrate areas of interest to the viewer, based on eye movement and dwell time.

Figure 11.1 Tracking the viewer's interest: a. gazeplot and b. heatspot

Storyboard and concept testing

Companies use computer-generated images to show versions of a potential advert. This cuts down on the expense of producing adverts. Respondents are asked to respond to the creative treatment and express their likelihood of purchasing.

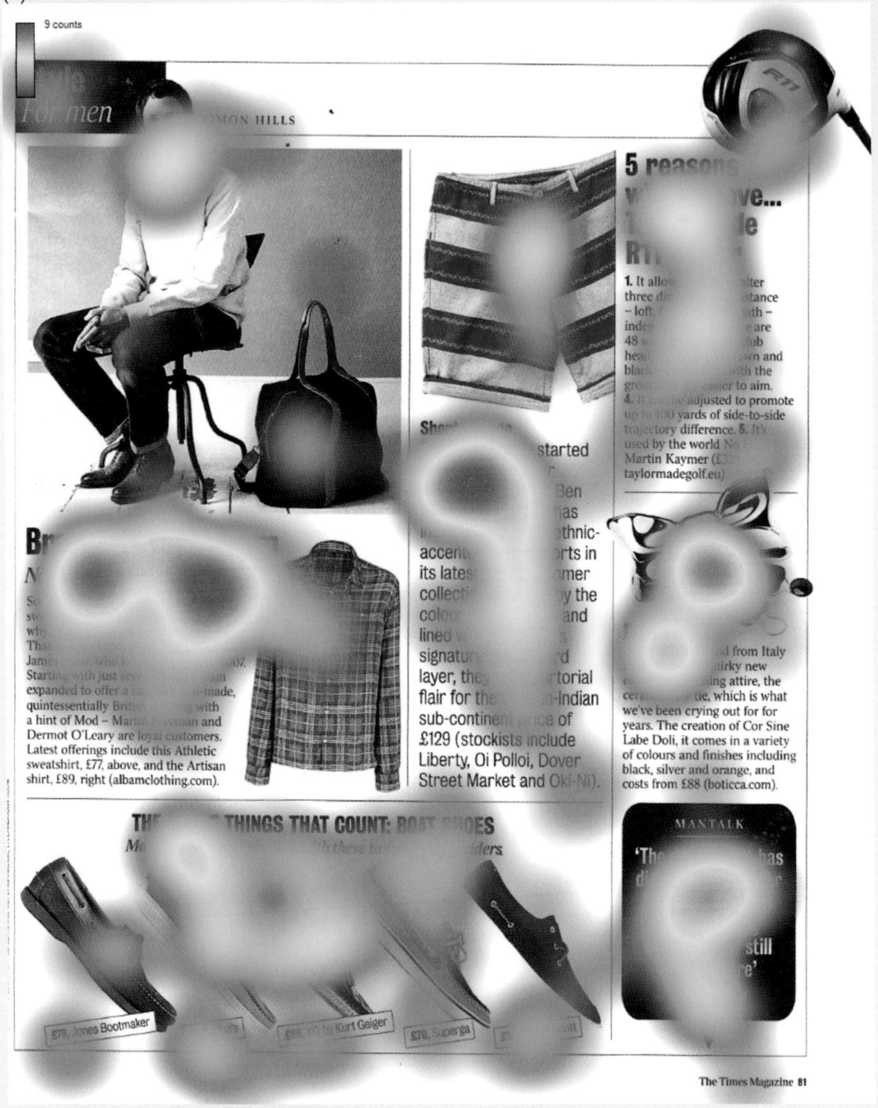

Figure 11.1 Continued

Consumer diaries

Consumer diaries vary depending on the type of data being collected. In the fashion industry, consumers are asked to keep a diary of their magazine reading and note any adverts or stories they were attracted to.

The camera in the television

Technology made it possible to place a camera in a television so that data can be collected on how the observer reacts to adverts, by paying attention, changing channels or leaving the room.

Projective techniques

Projective techniques ask the respondent to put themselves in a certain scenario:

- if money was no object
- if you needed an outfit for a certain event
- if you were a celebrity
- if you were size X.

This gives companies an insight into simple needs and more fanciful aspirations from which they can develop products and advertising treatments.

There are ways of investigating how consumers view, enjoy and remember advertising and promotion but we can never be sure that this will convert into purchasing.

CASE STUDY: Wasted advertising?

A friend told me that she was looking for a new winter coat and had seen an XYZ one that she really liked in an advert in a magazine but probably wouldn't buy it as she thought that everyone would have the same one! Is that a wasted advertising budget?

The following week, she was wearing a new winter coat and I asked 'did it come from XYZ?' 'Yes', she replied. She added that the coat she had seen in the advert had sold out and she liked this one better anyway. So the advertising wasn't wasted, was it?

Online research

Online research can be used to judge the effectiveness of communication campaigns. The advantage of web-based research is that it is quick and gives instant feedback. It can be used to test awareness of both online and offline promotions through online questionnaires as with traditional focus groups. Web-based interviewing can be used to access people who would otherwise be difficult to access, such as office-based consumers who would be reluctant to take part in street interviews or would not have the time to take part in focus groups.

Assessing the effectiveness of digital campaigns is done through web analytics and social media monitoring. Google analytics can give valuable data on 'clickthroughs' to web pages. Marketers can track blogs, YouTube and Facebook to get feedback on what consumers are saying about their brand. Social media monitoring at a simple level is about listening to consumer conversations across a range of digital platforms.

Boohoo.com is an Internet retailer that communicates solely online. Figure 11.2 demonstrates a combination of a vertical brick layout combined with colour shades to draw the viewer's eye through the whole communication as they scroll down. The e-mail is long but it includes many pictures, a little text and colourful graphics that flow diagonally down the page. This encourages viewers to spend much time on the images and maintain attention throughout.

Figure 11.3b shows very clearly that there are parts of the communication which the viewer almost completely ignores. Therefore it may not be as effective as other communications.

Costs of research

The costs of undertaking research can vary depending on the detail, sample size and number of variables to be explored, as well as the speed with which the research is required. If research is needed quickly then secondary sources may be sufficient as fieldwork or primary research will take longer and cost more.

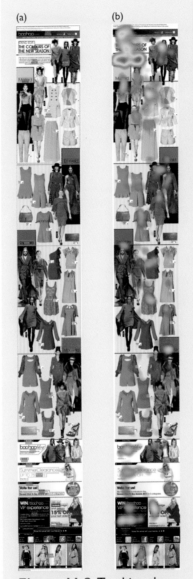

Figure 11.2 Tracking the viewer's interest: a. an e-mail and b. heatspots showing where the user looks

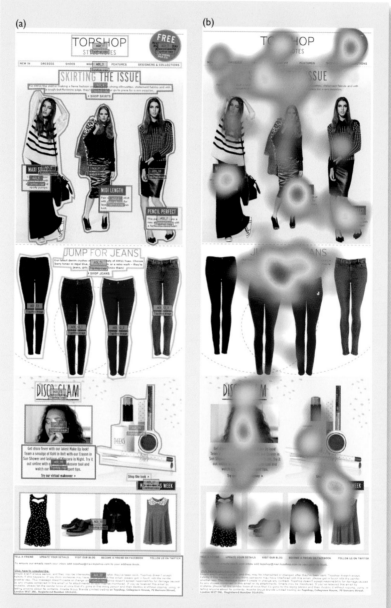

Figure 11.3 Losing the viewer's interest: a. an e-mail and
b. heatspots showing where the user looks

Summary

This chapter has established that, like most research into the complex workings of the human brain, purchasing behaviour can never be fully understood, however some techniques may give us some small insights. When it comes to fashion purchasing, the area is even more fraught with dangers as fashion is a very visible product where self-identity and self-esteem is mixed into the equation. Measuring advertising effectiveness is not a simple or exact science. Nevertheless, seeking to measure the effectiveness of any communications campaign is important if companies are to answer the age-old question of what they are getting for their money.

References

Mitchell, A. (2009) 'Unravel the mini-mysteries surrounding effectiveness', *Marketing*.

Morrison, M. A. *et al.* (2002) *Using Qualitative Research in Advertising*, Sage, London.

Activities

1. Access a selection of newspapers and fashion magazines and compare and contrast the messages in the brands being promoted.
2. Undertake a small-scale piece of qualitative research into consumers' awareness of high-street fashion advertising.
3. Join a research panel on the Internet (not necessarily about fashion) to gain an understanding of how consumer research is formulated.
4. Consider the Jaeger case study and answer the following questions:
   a. What could Coats Viyella have done to revitalise rather than divest the brand?
   b. What happened to Viyella?
   c. What sort of research would have been carried out to establish the perception of the brand prior to 2003–4?
   d. What types of research are appropriate for this investigation?
   e. Design some research tools to test consumer perceptions of Jaeger.
   f. What were the major objectives of Jaeger's integrated campaign?
   g. Which other people were involved in the repositioning of Jaeger?
   h. What aspects of the communications strategy were used and to what extent were they integrated into the repositioning strategy?
   i. Financial success is just one measure of effectiveness; what are other measures?
   j. How is Tillman 'doing a Jaeger' on Aquascutum?
   k. What is next for Jaeger now it has been restored to iconic British heritage brand status?

CASE STUDY: Jaeger

In the 1990s, Jaeger and Viyella were well-known clothing brands owned by the 200-year-old, British-based textile company, Coats Viyella. Coats Viyella was primarily a manufacturer of thread but it had diversified into manufacturing and fashion retail operating under the fascias Jaeger and Viyella. It also produced garments for leading high-street retailers, in particular Britain's major high-street chain Marks and Spencer (M&S). When M&S (in line with other British high-street retailers) made the strategic decision to move to off-shore sourcing, in the search for improved margins and economies of scale, the close relationship with Coats Viyella began to decline. M&S had been so closely linked with their suppliers that they were considered a major force in the structure of the UK fashion supply chain.

As a result of the loss of business, Coats Viyella found itself with two retail brands that they did not have the resources to support. The parent company made the decision to dispose of these two retail brands and focus more on the global thread business. At the time of the disposal, Jaeger was a loss-making enterprise with an uncertain image and few strong brand assets outside of its central London store in Regent Street. The main retail outlets at the time of the sale were 52 stores supported by 94 concessions. It was a brand in need of revitalisation.

You're always ten years too young for Jaeger.

—*Belinda Earl, Chief Executive, Jaeger, 2004*

Jaeger had suffered from underinvestment. It had lost its direction and even its core loyal customer base, despite having hired Bella Freud, a top international designer who had been brought in to try and spice up the brand image. The company was sold for £1 to Riverhawk, which sold Jaeger, within weeks, to Harold Tillman, the high-profile chairman of the British Fashion Council, who said 'I got it for a good price, I never over pay for anything' (Tillman, 2004). Tillman's CV reads like a timeline of acquisitions and divestments; he also purchased Aquascutum in 2009.

(Continued)

Research before Repositioning

Tillman employed MediaCom, one of the world's leading integrated media agencies, to find out what past, present and potential customers of Jaeger thought of the brand. Consumer research was undertaken in 2003–4, at the time of acquisition, and in 2007, during a repositioning programme. The finding of the initial research was that the Jaeger brand was perceived by UK consumers as high-priced merchandise appealing to women over 40, offering classic ranges but with little fashion content. This was at a time when new entrants, both national and international, were entering the market or strengthening their market position. The UK high-street chain NEXT was gaining market share; new entrants, such as Sweden's H&M and Spain's Zara, were gaining a foothold in the market and introducing innovative fashion ranges. Fast fashion was gaining a following on the British high street and was rapidly changing consumer perceptions of affordability.

By 2007, the market perception of Jaeger was that it was high priced but more fashion led. It was attracting some younger customers but this was a confused picture and customers commented that fashionable products were sometimes mixed in with long-standing classics and store environments were uninspiring. However, the overall finding was that the message that Jaeger had changed was not reaching the customers, the media or the market.

The Repositioning Process

In response, the company set about differentiating its sub-brands. These sub-brands had the following positioning strategies:

- Jaeger: core merchandise
- London: directional fashion
- Black: premium range

The major focus of the repositioning exercise was an emphasis on accessories, thus allowing potential customers to buy into the brand at entry price level. A handbag was the vehicle for this. The 'Tilly' was launched in 2008, priced at £299, and quickly became an 'it' bag. A separate bag, 'Miranda', was launched as the Jaeger London bag at £599.

(Continued)

The old logo, which had depicted the warp and weft of wool reflecting the Coats company origins as a manufacturer, was dropped and a new logo designed to convey an image of modernity (see Figure 11.4).

Figure 11.4 Jaeger logos: old and new

Prior to 2008, all Jaeger media promotion was handled in-house and consisted mostly of newspaper advertising in the quality broadsheets. The in-house communication team was enhanced by the arrival of luxury media specialists Red, at an annual cost of £500,000. The media focus shifted to advertising in *Vogue*, *Grazia* and *Tatler*, the top-end fashion magazines. Spending on advertising in these magazines and other high-profile media channels was reinforced with PR campaigns and celebrity endorsement.

A coat worn by Davina McCall on the popular TV programme *Big Brother* sold out immediately; Emma Thompson, a famous character actress, often wore the brand to awards ceremonies; Erin O'Connor, a top model, was made the new face of Jaeger. The power of celebrity endorsement could be seen when the star print blouse, worn by supermodel Kate Moss, increased sales by 300%. Above all, it was the 'Tilly' bag which secured the most PR coverage.

Securing spots at London Fashion Week in Spring and Autumn 2008 and the consequent press coverage also gave the brand a cachet that had been lacking before repositioning. Jaeger was hailed by some of the British fashion press (such as *Vogue*) as 'the return of the iconic British super-brand'. Belinda

(Continued)

Earl, the new chief executive was credited with turning Jaeger's ailing brand status around.

Customer retention was improved through the introduction of a loyalty card and in-store magazines, which gave customers something back and built a stronger brand affiliation. Launching an online transactional website proved to be effective in widening Jaeger's geographic reach, when new stores were no longer being opened. The website also increased international exposure, which lead to many overseas store openings.

Stores were refurbished and the Regent Street flagship store became just that once more, with a million-pound refit. Sales personnel did not and were not obliged to wear pieces from the Jaeger range until 2007; indeed, Belinda Earl admitted that when she joined Jaeger she 'struggled' to find something to wear.

Research after Repositioning

After the repositioning process, consumer research suggested that custom-ers were younger and less likely to think of Jaeger as a brand for older customers. A concession opened in Selfridges. Consumers cited the bag and statement jewellery ranges as the changes which made them reconsider the brand although the price of the bag was deemed too cheap by some to be considered as an 'it' bag, for which they would expect to pay £500.

Consumers were able to name the celebrities associated with Jaeger. In those stores that had been refurbished, the store environment was praised. Raised awareness of the brand through magazines was mentioned. Jaeger was seen to be attracting younger sales staff, which would suggest that Jaeger was proving to be a brand that a younger consumer was happy to be seen in.

Between 2004 and 2008 turnover showed year on year increases, but so did expenditure (Bell 2009).

Jaeger would appear to have been restored to its rightful status as an iconic British heritage brand, just like its competitors Burberry and Mulberry.

(Continued)

The Current Market Position

By 2011, the company had more than 40 stores in the UK and had turned its attention to overseas markets. In 2009, Paris was identified as a potential target destination. This would be a return entry for the brand, which had a presence in the city in the 1960s – as the brand began to decline, international operations had been scaled back.

At the beginning of 2011, Jaeger was looking at Russia in collaboration with a Russian luxury brand distributor, Jamilco, whose president said, 'Jaeger has global appeal and we are positive that Russian consumers will appreciate the brand's heritage of noble fibres and unique designs' (Gallagher 2011).

References

Bell, K. (2009) MSc thesis.

Gallagher, V. (2011) 'Jaeger to expand into Russia', *Retail Week*, 10 February 2011.

Jaeger, www.Jaeger.co.uk.

MediaCom, www.MediaCom.co.uk.

Tillman, H. (2004) *Director*, October 2004.

FUTURE DIRECTIONS IN FASHION MARKETING COMMUNICATIONS

I never think of the future. It comes soon enough.

—Albert Einstein

THIS CHAPTER:

- brings together some of the most recent developments and observations in fashion marketing communications

- suggests career directions for students who aspire to work in the industry.

Introduction

During the time that this book was being written, much was subtly changing in the fashion communications arena. Digital marketing tools became a mainstay of fashion marketing communications; although some commentators suggested the demise of traditional tools, this has not been the case. The traditional tools, such as advertising, magazines and the retail environment, have instead become an integrated multi-channel medium for communication.

This chapter points more specifically to those developments and gives some advice on careers in the industry, at what is an exciting time.

The changing landscape of media communications

The activity and spending on traditional marketing communications (TV, magazines etc.) has remained stagnant or reduced slightly in the last five years in the economic downturn, but so have prices for these media. More channels have become available on satellite TV.

Online content, mobile media and social media, driven by PR, has increased. These are seen as almost invisible aspects of costing. These media channels are often calculated in a different way to that of traditional channels, as they can come in under a variety of budgets including sales and marketing. The allocation of media budgets of these areas is often a somewhat grey area.

Most magazines now have an online version. It is not envisaged at this stage that online versions will usurp traditional glossy fashion magazines, which contain longer features more suited to the reader perusing at leisure. Online content provides short sharp bursts of updated information and reminds the customer to buy the magazine. To date, most fashion magazines have not made a charge for access to online content. This may change.

Technological advances

Mobile media (accessible via smart phones) now appears to be reaching critical mass as the devices have dropped in price and have been adopted by the majority of the target market for fashion, that is the 18 to 35 year old consumer.

Owners of smart phones take their 'personal access devices' with them and would be lost without them as these provide constant updates. The smart phone is also their 'in-hand', highly portable lifeline, their diary, their camera and their e-mail and social media portal. It is a vital part of their engagement with communications and serves as an infotainment centre.

Static traditional adverts in magazines or on ambient media may contain quick response (QR) codes. When an interested consumer scans the code on a mobile device, it links directly to the company website where they can get information on trends and, more importantly, shop immediately using m-commerce. To date, QR codes are not attractive visually; they look quite clumsy at times and will certainly evolve in the future.

Applications, better known as 'apps', downloaded by the customer give immediate direct access and constant updates to whatever site the customer has chosen. It has been widely predicted in the fashion and technological press that mobile phones will soon be used as payment devices. They will be able to be loaded with credit and payment will be made by passing them over a till terminal.

Augmented reality or augmented browsing can be used in magazine advertising or editorial features to link the viewer to further expanded content, images or information.

Social media sites, such as Facebook, facilitate a 24/7 sharing platform for whatever consumers want to say to their friends. The site clearly uses search engine optimisation and browsing history (brand mentions) to target adverts at the consumer who has shown some interest in a brand; more often, a competing brand will pop up in the advertising section. These adverts become less intrusive as they are for brands that the consumer has actively sought out or to which they would be attracted. For example, I mentioned UGG boots in an ostensibly private post on Facebook and was immediately targeted by EMU (a direct competitor) on my Facebook pop-up adverts.

Rich media and infotainment

Website banner ads, which were originally quite static, have been revitalised by 'rich media'. They are more engaging and eye catching; they encourage engagement.

Fashion websites are increasingly embedding online video content as infotainment, turning users into viewers. The next stage of this will be the ability to click and buy from a catwalk.

In the retail environment, interactive mirrors and direct links with live streaming via tablets at the point of sale will show the full range in a small store environment. This means that retailers in small units in satellite towns will be able to showcase a wider range of goods than the range they can afford to stock. This ticks a couple of sustainability boxes: the consumer does not need to travel to a city centre and allows shops located on the local high street to cater for the fashion consumer.

Blogs

Blogging has become the fashion commentary of the moment. A blog was originally called a 'web log'; it is a diary-style website with thoughts, comments and visual images. Blogging is active and interactive. Web 2.0 technology facilitates a two-way conversation that incorporates comments and encourages followers.

Bloggers are the new influential fashion journalists of today. They frequent the front rows of fashion shows bringing up-to-date visuals and commentary faster than a traditional journalist ever could.

Monetising the Internet is not easy to quantify. Affiliate marketing is the new pyramid selling — bloggers are paid every time a viewer clicks on embedded or overt advertising content in their blog. To the untrained eye, a recommendation by a blogger is often seen as impartial but many bloggers are paid to review products favourably and have overt advertising on their websites. Bloggers are also paid to style fashion shoots for retailers, contribute to columns in magazines and newspapers and comment on celebrity styles and the industry.

In an attempt to be more transparent, the most famous street fashion and style bloggers (such as Garance Doré shown in Figure 12.1) have announced that this is how they earn their living.

As this part of the communications industry is becoming more mainstream (no business could survive without at least a rudimentary website), the opportunities for digital practitioners have been building momentum.

Figure 12.1 Influential blog: Garance Doré

Career opportunities

There are various routes into careers in fashion marketing communications, not all of them straightforward by any means. It needs resilience, drive and application by the individual. The roles and responsibilities can vary widely across the industry in different companies, advertising agencies or in-house creative departments.

Working in advertising may not mean solely working on fashion brands. Should opportunities arise, it will certainly help if your studies at college or university have included the history of fashion, fashion theory, journalism, photography, fashion promotion, styling, visual merchandising or fashion marketing communications set in the wider context of retail fashion marketing.

Many advertising and marketing communications agencies have specialist areas that focus on luxury, lifestyle and beauty brands. Others deal in a single sector, such as the home-shopping market. Red C is a marketing agency that focusses on the home-shopping market. It says (2011):

Retail is at a crucial crossroads right now, in the doom and gloom of the economic downturn, some of the traditional big-spending UK marketers are in trouble. Retailers are succumbing to depressed High Street spending in record numbers – Woolworths, MFI, Whittards, Zavvi, Adams – and predictions are for several more high profile casualties this year.

It's no surprise that retailers are turning to relationship marketing techniques to survive, and that's where Red C can help. We believe that the successful businesses will be those that can find the right balance between their physical presence and their online activity. Why should retailers continue to pay high property rentals when they can reach customers, perhaps far more effectively, online?

Of course, there are flaws in this argument. We can't yet substitute the vital impact of eye contact and dialogue in the physical shop environment within our e-commerce emporia. So instead we focus on improving your ROI and sales per square foot through such techniques such as catchment area penetration strategies, turning around under-performing stores and improving store POS. If your current marketing isn't getting the impact and results you need, you should be talking to us.

Work experience

The value of work experience cannot be underestimated. Longer placements, of up to a year, may be paid (see Figure 12.2); short ones are normally unpaid. These positions have become known as 'internships'. To date, despite government threats of legislation regarding unpaid placements and work experience, many students view an internship as an opportunity. There are a number of websites devoted to the positive and negative aspects of these opportunities. Most successful graduates have undertaken placements of one form or another. They say that it was hard work at the time and involved many sacrifices but was instrumental in their career. If you do not have any experience, get some as soon as possible even if it is only a short, even a week-long, placement shadowing in a company.

Company: ZPR
Role: PR Assistant (Fashion & Beauty)
Location: London, W1D 4SH
Salary: £16,000 per annum
Duration: 13 months
Start: 18th June 2011
Deadline: 11th May 2012

Company Profile

ZPR is a PR company based in Soho, London which specialises in consumer PR for retailers. ZPR provides communications support to a number of major retailers including Waitrose, Superdrug, Lakeland, B&Q and smaller niche brands such as Vevie and The Essential One. ZPR has also recently been involved in a number of new business pitches to expand on its fashion accounts.

We are looking for a student to work across our fashion and beauty accounts starting from 4th June 2011.

Role Outline

The role will include:
- Managing our sample process for product placement PR opportunities in national press
- Keeping up to date with the media and collating media and coverage reports
- Research
- Administration
- Liaising with journalists for product placement opportunities
- Writing press releases
- Drafting product flashes
- Helping with press events
- Store visits
- Liaising with H/O for product/price enquiries
- Maintaining a good overall image

Person Specification
- We are looking for someone who has a genuine interest in fashion, beauty and lifestyle.
- You must have an eye for style/fashion.
- You must have excellent written and verbal communication skills
- You must be organised and confident.
- You must be flexible and approach every task with a positive 'can do' attitude.
- You must be a willing team player who is capable of working in a fast pace environment.
- We are keen that they already have relations/friends in London as starting a placement and not knowing anyone in London can be quite daunting

Figure 12.2 Advertisement for a paid year-long internship

Hilary Alexander, formerly fashion editor at *The Telegraph* shared her top tips for interns with me:

> I get the prospective interns to write something, anything, that they are passionate about. If they can't spell or punctuate ... it goes in the bin, but if they can and are passionate, they come for two weeks and if then they are enthusiastic and show initiative, they can stay longer. Some stay a week, some stay forever.

To gain work experience, you can use the companies that your educational institution has already on their contacts list or you can identify companies you would like to work for and make contact on your own.

The case study is a statement from someone working in a luxury brand. He outlines his educational background and the work experience he undertook to get to where he is today.

CASE STUDY: One man's experience

I currently work as a supervisor and client relationship management executive for a French luxury fashion house known for its visionary founder, haute couture and continuously reinvented timeless looks.

I started my career in fashion marketing communications rather unknowingly at the age of 16 when I decided to get a weekend job in a branch of a rather well-known, high-street shoe retailer that had opened in my local town, whilst finishing my school years. As I gained experience of what it entailed being on the shop floor, I decided that the industry was much more than just selling products: it was about creating a lifestyle and selling a 'vision' to clients.

One year into my 'career', if you can call it that at such an early stage, I was approached to work for a local brand who had recently gained a loyal fan base and had taken their image and message global. The task was to work

(Continued)

with a small team to help set up and run a trial flagship retail store for said brand, and help them create a retail image that they would use on their quest to become market leaders in the street or urban fashion field. Our job was to ensure the 'right' people heard about our brand, convert them into 'followers' and make sure that they were only shopping in our store and, most importantly, make our brand parties legendary! At this time, social media was not what it is today – only a few people that I knew had a Bebo page, Zuckerberg hadn't even thought of connecting people at this point, so our strategy was old fashioned 'word of mouth', not today's 'cyber word of mouth'.

Whilst gaining this exciting experience and being offered a permanent position with the brand, I understood the importance of academic studies, and as such continued with my BTEC business course at college. I only attended college three days a week, meaning I had four days to work on the project.

Once I had completed my college years, I decided to carry on my academic studies by opting to go to university. It took me a long time to choose the right course as I wanted something that was primarily based around business but also allowed me to develop the experience I had gained while working with the street label in my home town. I found a course perfect for what I was looking for: international fashion marketing, a business and marketing degree centred around fashion; further more, it was based in Cottonopolis (Manchester, the birthplace of the clothing industry as we know it today!).

As soon as I had unpacked in Manchester, I set about finding a part-time job which would allow me to keep the same routine which I had back home; that was, to learn while being actively involved in a business. I was employed as a sales assistant for an Italian luxury goods brand which had recently opened a concession in Selfridges. Many of my friends dismissed the idea of 'only working as a sales assistant', but I thrived on the opportunity to work for a large, well-known company and gain knowledge of their clientele and how these brands run their ever-increasing democratised luxury fashion empires!

The third year of my degree saw me complete a compulsory year of industry work placement. I joined a small, luxury, personal training business in

(Continued)

London with a view to assisting them research, develop and sell a high-end performance clothing label in the UK sportswear market. The fact that I had worked for a reputable luxury fashion house made me stand out from my peers who had dismissed the idea of working in retail. I believe this work placement developed my business acumen, time discipline and determination to succeed more than anything else I had done in the past, as I was entrusted with many important tasks such as briefing design teams, dealing with suppliers and conducting sales meetings with large retailers. I attribute to the discipline, confidence and motivation boosting me to completing my studies by achieving a first-class honours degree once I returned to university.

Whilst finishing their studies, many of my peers, who had not been keen on working part-time, were even less motivated to do so due to the large amount of work required to achieve a good degree classification. I on the other hand, increased my work hours to 24 hours a week and set about completing my degree and building on that invaluable experience.

I, as all graduates who obtained a good classification and the motivation to go forth and conquer our chosen industry and become the next stars of the future, set out to find the perfect job! However this proved more of a task than I had first thought, and after two months of searching with no return, I found myself working as a full-time sales assistant for a French luxury brand, something which I had not set out to do. I felt deflated and longed to be doing something more challenging, however my knowledge of the industry and my business-minded approach to my work saw me being placed in the UK flagship within six months and promoted to supervisor and client relations management executive with the task of developing a framework for all staff to follow in order to help them and the business develop new clients and nurture these clients in an ever competitive market place.

I am responsible for executing the effectiveness of physical layout and provisions of customer service and improving processes within our boutique. The project I am currently working on is in preparation for the launch of a new larger boutique opening 2013 in London where we will expand to more than 100 team members. It will be the second largest boutique outside of

(Continued)

Paris and will be regarded as one of the most luxurious boutiques not only in London, but the world.

The only advice that I can give to anyone looking for a way into fashion marcoms is that there is no set path to follow. Everyone has their own way of making it into the industry. Some may achieve it quicker than others, but I believe determination, hard work and being positive with a down-to-earth attitude will get you there! Always put 100% effort into everything you do, be it a conversation with a client, a meeting, or even the coffee making and you will be recognised.

Top tips

Following these tips will help you gain a work placement or a permanent role:

- Research, research, and then do more research.
- There are many companies that you may never have heard of as they are not high-street names. They may be international players with holding company names. Just because they are not recognisable to you immediately, you should not dismiss them.
- Responding to an advert for a job, you should ensure that you match the criteria and the key words used in the advert. These should be reflected back to the company to demonstrate how your experience matches their job specification.
- Many candidates expect the reader to pick through a wealth of random experience and make connections which fit the job description. In a competitive marketplace, the reader will not do this.
- Ensure that you know the company and their products, prices, distribution channels and promotional tactics. In order to work in fashion marketing communications, you have to understand the total company ethos and marketing mix, locally and internationally, not just their promotional tools.
- Visit the store in a number of locations at different times. Far too many applicants for job roles have never visited the store but rely on the

website for information. This is biased data and can never give a true in-store experience.

↳ Interrogate the website fully and sign up for their e-mails or social media and then monitor the activity.

↳ Carry out a structured analysis on the company of your choice, which may include a PEST and SWOT (including a competitor) analysis that takes in the macro and micro variables impacting on their business. Companies often ask you to use this research as part of a presentation.

The interview process

Some interviews are formal, with a panel of three; some are quite informal, one-to-one discussions over a coffee. Find out which one you will have; if you cannot, be prepared for either type.

Formal applications require a CV and sometimes a cover letter. More often now, you may have to fill in an online application, which you should complete with your CV and cover letter in mind.

Many companies will require a presentation. When preparing a presentation, you should:

↳ keep the number of words on a slide to a minimum
↳ practice what you have to say
↳ talk naturally using the slides as prompts rather than cue cards.

Companies may also use assessment centres and 'live' tasks to select candidates. You will be in a small group, asked to solve a problem in a set time frame. This shows you are either a team player or you are not. Listen to other candidates as well as trying to get your point across. You will be observed by the company representatives.

Blogs and websites have become increasingly popular as a selection tool. The company may ask you to start one of your own and they will monitor it. Companies also use search engines – they will look at your Facebook profile picture, so make sure it is professional.

After an interview, most companies are happy to give feedback and this should guide you for the future.

References

Amed, I. (2011) 'The Business of Blogging: The Sartorialist', available at www.businessoffash
ion.com /2011/10/the-business-of-blogging-the-sartorialist.html [Accessed 1 May 2012].

Red C (2011) *Our Big Book of Credentials*, p. 36, available at www.redcmarketing.net/wp-
content/themes/redc/6_pdfs/Red_C_Credentials.pdf [Accessed 1 May 2012].

Activities

1   Mention a brand in a Facebook post and see how you are targeted by them or their competitors.
2   What future fashion marketing communications and applications can you envisage?
3   Identify an advert for a job of your choice. Make a note of the key words they use. Write a targeted cover letter and CV.
4   Prepare a presentation for the role.

INDEX